HOTSPOTS
CORFU

GW00631065

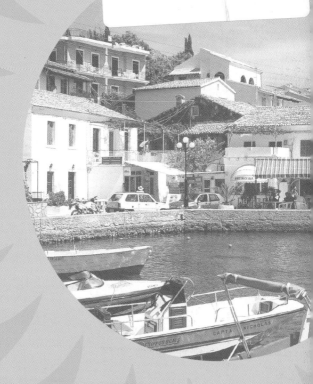

Written by Kerry Fisher, updated by Mike Gerrard
Front cover photography courtesy of Thomas Cook Tour Operations Ltd

Original concept by Studio 183 Limited
Series design by the Bridgewater Book Company
Cover design/artwork by Lee Biggadike, Studio 183 Limited

Produced by the Bridgewater Book Company
The Old Candlemakers, West Street, Lewes, East Sussex BN7 2NZ, United Kingdom
www.bridgewaterbooks.co.uk
Project Editor: Emily Casey Bailey
Project Designer: Lisa McCormick

Published by Thomas Cook Publishing
A division of Thomas Cook Tour Operations Limited
PO Box 227, Units 15-16, Coningsby Road, Peterborough PE3 8SB, United Kingdom
email: books@thomascook.com
www.thomascookpublishing.com
+ 44 (0) 1733 416477

ISBN-13: 978-1-84157-535-3
ISBN-10: 1-84157-535-6

First edition © 2006 Thomas Cook Publishing
Text © 2006 Thomas Cook Publishing
Maps © 2006 Thomas Cook Publishing
Head of Thomas Cook Publishing: Chris Young
Project Editor: Diane Ashmore
Production/DTP Editor: Steven Collins

Printed and bound in Spain by Graficas Cems, Navarra, Spain

CONTENTS

SYMBOLS KEY

The following is a key to the symbols used throughout this book:

church   shopping   bar

bus stop   restaurant   fine dining

tip   café

O telephone   **F** fax   **e** email   **W** website address

a address   **L** opening times   **O** important

€ budget price   €€ mid-range price   €€€ most expensive

★ specialist interest   ★★ see if passing   ★★★ top attraction

---

Getting to know Corfu

Corfu is the northernmost of the Ionian islands and the second largest in the group. It lies just off the west coast of the Greek mainland and only a few kilometres from Albania. In the shape of a sickle, it is about 64 km (40 miles) long and 29 km (18 miles) across. Despite its relatively small size, this olive-tree-covered island encompasses a variety of vegetation, architecture and activities to delight and fascinate visitors.

THE MYTHICAL ISLAND

Corfu is known as Kerkyra in Greek. Legend has it that the name comes from a nymph called Korkyra, who was brought to the island by her lover, Poseidon, the god of the sea. In ancient Greek literature, Homer refers to Corfu as the home of the Phaeacians, also calling it Scheria. In the Odyssey, he mentions the island when recounting the story of *Odysseus* who was shipwrecked on his way home to Ithaca. He was washed up on a beach before being rescued by the beautiful Princess Nausicaa. Paleokastritsa is the top contender for the beach in question, although several others, like Ermones, also stake a claim.

HISTORICAL CORFU

Although the island has adapted to accommodate the tourist market, with English breakfasts, Cornish pasties and trendy brands of beer, Corfu remains essentially Greek, with a delightful combination of other cultural influences. Its position between Greece and Italy made it a sought-after maritime stronghold, occupied by various nations over the centuries. The architecture on the island today is a legacy of its chequered past.

Nowhere is this more obvious than in Corfu Town itself, where elegant Venetian houses line a labyrinth of narrow alleys and the arcaded French-built Liston stands metres from the imposing British palace of St Michael and St George.

The inquisitive visitor who peeps behind the modern facade of hotels and bars will encounter exquisite monasteries, churches, ruined castles and an array of museums that chart the island's rich history.

The best of Corfu

BEACHES

Pebble, shingle, sandy, lively, deserted or only accessible by boat, Corfu's coastline encompasses every sort of beach. The secluded coves of **Liapades** (see page 43) and **Agni** (see page 67) are wonderful for chilling out with a book, with the odd foray into crystal-clear water to cool off. For sandy beaches, the wide stretches of terracotta sands at **Aghios Georgios** (south-west, see page 27 – and north-west, see page 46), **Glyfada** (see page 34) and **Aghios Stefanos** (see page 50) are hard to beat. If you want at least 100 m (109 yd) between you and the next person, head for the near-deserted sand dunes on the shores of **Lake Korission** (see page 27). Spectacular scenery is the backdrop to **Sunset Beach**, near Sidari (see page 55), and to **Aghios Gordios**, on the west coast (see page 31). **Dassia** (see page 76), **Kavos** (see page 24) and **Ipsos** (see page 72) are all top spots for trying out parascending or water-skiing.

SIGHTSEEING

It's difficult to pick out one attraction from the many enchanting sights in **Corfu Town** (see page 10). The **Achilleion Palace** (see page 86) is worth a look for the over-the-top decoration, beautiful gardens and the Dying Achilles statue. The **Paleokastritsa Monastery** (see page 44) has a peaceful atmosphere, as well as lovely terraces and views. The peak of **Mount Pantokrator** (see page 61) is the ultimate on-top-of-the-world sensation.

OFF THE BEATEN TRACK

Beautiful walks include the flower-scented path up to the chapel at **Aghios Stefanos** (see page 51) and past the lemon groves and through the narrow alleyways to the **Monastery of Christ Pantokrator** at **Aghios Markos** (near Ipsos – see page 72). The hill villages of **Spartilas** and **Strinilas** (see page 73) are good starting or finishing points for exploring the lower slopes of **Mount Pantokrator**. The pretty harbour of **Kouloura** (see page 73) is an idyllic destination for walks from Kalami, Krouseri and Agni beaches.

RESORTS
Places under the sun

Corfu Town
Venetian character and charm

Every narrow alley or arcaded street in the island's capital offers up a host of entrancing images. The Venetians ruled Corfu from 1386 to 1797 and the architecture has a strong Italian influence, with little squares and ornate wells nestling below elegant churches and bell towers.

THINGS TO SEE & DO

Aghios Spyridon Church ★★★

This red-domed church is dedicated to the shepherd-turned-bishop who is credited with saving the island from many disasters, not least the Turkish siege in 1716. His remains, smuggled on a donkey from Constantinople to Corfu in the 15th century, are in a silver reliquary to the right of the altar. ❷ One block behind the Liston in Aghios Spyridon Square ❶ 26610 33059 ❸ Open 09.00–14.00 ❶ Donations welcome

Archaeological Museum ★★★

This airy museum contains a wealth of finds, including funerary urns, bronze statues and a 6th-century BC stone lion. ❷ 5 Vraila ❶ 26610 30680 ❸ Open Tues–Sun 08.30–15.00, closed Mon ❶ Admission charge

British Cemetery ★

This peaceful oasis, dating from the 19th century, is dotted with lily ponds and palm trees and overflows with wild orchids in the spring. The road past the cemetery brings you to the mid-19th-century prison, which is still used today. From here, you can walk downhill to Garitsa bay. ❷ South of San Rocco Square ❸ Open daily

The Byzantine Museum ★★

The restored church of Antivouniotissa houses a collection of religious artefacts, majestic silver candelabra and 15th- to 19th-century icons. It

---

❶ *The red dome of Aghios Spyridon church rises high over Corfu Town*

has a beautiful garden at the back, complete with bell tower. ⓐ In the Church of Antivouniotissa, off Arseniou Street, up the steps ⓘ 26610 38313 🕒 Open Tues–Sun 08.30–15.00, closed Mon ❶ Admission charge

Church of St Jason and St Sosipater ★

Walking back from Mon Repos to Corfu Town, a left turn before the Marina Hotel leads you to the 10th- to 11th-century octagonal-domed Byzantine church, dedicated to two of St Paul's disciples, credited with bringing Christianity to Corfu around AD 48. 🕒 Open daily, all day

The Liston ★★★

The Liston is an arcaded promenade built in 1807 on the instructions of Napoleon as an imitation of the Parisian Rue de Rivoli. Its name is derived from the Venetian *libro d'oro*, an exclusive golden book listing the names of the aristocrats who were allowed to walk here. It still has a stylish air about it, and is filled with cafés and restaurants.

Mon Repos Park and Villa ★★

The access to this pretty wooded park is through green iron gates, opposite the ruined Palaiopolis basilica. It was built for the British High Commissioner, Frederic Adam, in 1824 and later served as a summer residence for the Greek royal family. Prince Philip, Duke of Edinburgh, was born here in 1921. The restored villa is open to the public as the very enjoyable Palaiopolis Museum. 🕒 Grounds open 08.00–19.00; museum Tues–Sun 08.30–15.00 ❶ Grounds free; admission charge for museum

The New Fortress ★★

Overlooking the marina in the old town, the new fortress was built by the Venetians in 1576 to strengthen the town's defences after one of many attacks by the Turks. You can climb to the top for views over the town and across the sea to Albania. There is also a cool, stone café with arrow slits for windows. ⓐ The entrance is just after the Tenedos church in Solomos Street 🕒 Open 09.00–21.00, depending on the season ❶ Small admission charge

The **Greek Orthodox Cathedral of the Blessed Virgin Mary** in the old part of town, facing the square of the harbour, is a favourite spot for weddings during the summer. Look out for immaculately attired guests enthusiastically hurling handfuls of rice at the happy couple.

The Old Fortress ★★★

Defences were constructed on the twin peaks of the fortress as early as the 6th century. Most of the fortifications there today were built by the Venetians in the 15th and 16th centuries. Climb up to the top for wonderful views. ⓐ Entrance from the Esplanade Square ⓛ Open Tues–Sun 08.30–15.00, longer in summer ⓘ Admission charge

Palace of St Michael and St George ★★★

Built in neo-classical British style between 1819 and 1824, it was originally the residence of Sir Thomas Maitland, the first British High Commissioner. It is now a very impressive museum of Asiatic art. You can also see the state rooms, which are very grand. ⓐ Esplanade (Spianada) northern end ⓛ Open Tues–Sun 08.30–15.00 ⓘ Admission charge

Boat trip ★★

Book a trip on the *Kalypso Star* and experience the wonderful world beneath the sea through bay windows. There's also an excellent underwater show with sea lions and a diver. ⓣ 26610 46525 ⓘ See your holiday representative for more details

RESTAURANTS & BARS (see map on page 15)

Aegli €€–€€€ ❶ The perfect place for watching chic Corfiots sashay by. Serves a mixture of Greek specialities and innovative cuisine. ⓐ 23 Kapodistriou Street, at the Palace end of the Liston ⓣ 26610 31949 ⓛ Open for lunch and dinner

Art Café €€ ❷ Newly fashionable hang-out, with outdoor seating and a 1930s-style interior. ⓐ Behind the Palace of St Michael and St George ⓣ 26610 49366

Café Grec €€ ❸ A little, slightly quieter place, popular with locals. ⓐ Palace end of Liston ❶ 26610 36645

 Il Giardino €€ ❹ Classy and intimate. Delicious Italian dishes are served in the shade of a large orange tree. ⓐ Opposite the Archaeological Museum ❶ 26610 30723 ⓒ Open evenings only

🍸 **Hotel Cavalieri** €€€ ❺ Splash out on a cocktail or ice cream on the candlelit roof terrace of this swish hotel – the views are stunning. ⓐ 4 Kapodistriou Street ❶ 26610 39041

 Magnet €–€€ ❻ Upbeat bar and café hang-out for young people. ⓐ Palace end of the Liston ❶ 26610 45295 ⓒ Open 18.00–01.00

SHOPPING

Shoppers will find all the olive wood, jewellery and clothes they can carry west of the Spianada, and on picturesque, arcaded Nikiforou Theotoki Street. In early morning, head to the fruit and vegetable market in the moat of the new fortress for a slice of tue Corfiot life. Later in the day, try visiting these shops:

Rosie's Bakery Traditional sweets made without eggs or butter which will last up to 15 days, making unusual treats.
ⓐ 71 Palaiologou ❶ 02915 6573

Hercules Vlachos This shop looks to Greek museum pieces for inspiration, with replicas of ancient sculptures and elaborate embroideries, plus affordable glass bowls, kitchenware and brass door knockers. ⓐ 82 Kapodistriou Street ❶ 26610 39024

Kallyndron Chunky handmade silver jewellery, shoes from Bali, wind chimes and summer dresses. ⓐ 61 Nikiforou Theotoki Street ❶ 26610 47434

Terracotta A good place for unusual jewellery, wall hangings and statues by Greek artists. ⓐ 2 Filarmonikis Street ❶ 26610 45260

MEDITERRANEAN SEA

N

| 0 | | 200 m |
| 0 | | 500 ft |

The Old
Fortress

Garitsa
Bay

2 PALACE OF ST MICHAEL
AND ST GEORGE

**CORFU
TOWN**

3

THE LISTON

KAPODISTRIOU

5

AKADIMIAS

6 Old
Town

1

GUILFORD

RARTOUROU

BYZANTINE
MUSEUM

AGHIOS
SPYRIDON

ARCHAEOLOGICAL
MUSEUM

DIMOKRATIAS

TOWN HALL

CATHEDRAL

4

N THEOTOKI

PALEOLOGOU

VOULGAREOS

CHURCH OF
ST JASON &
ST SOSIPATER,
MON REPOS

ALEXANDRAS

VELISSARIOU

G THEOTOKI

BRITISH
CEMETERY

The New
Fortress

I THEOTOKI

LEFKIMIS

Perama
attractive sightseeing base

Situated halfway between the island's capital and the lively seaside village of Benitses, Perama lies on the steep shoreline south of Corfu Town amongst lush green vegetation.

THINGS TO SEE & DO
Aghios Ioannis ★

Just south of Benitses (see below) is the resort of **Aghios Ioannis** (**St John's**) with its clean, sandy beach and plenty of water activities on offer, including round-the-island boat trips. There are some good tavernas, including the **Marbella Fish Taverna** (€–€€) on the main street just before the tunnel and the Melia Marbella Hotel. **La Terrazza** (€€–€€€) restaurant at the Melia Marbella has superb views across the sea and towards Corfu Town. There is a regular green bus service to Corfu Town – about half an hour's journey.

Analipsis ★

Visit Analipsis, whose spring used to supply fresh water to Venetian ships. The spring is now a trickle and the inscription says those who drink from it will never see their homeland again! Carry on down the path to a tiny cove for a dip. The largest part of the top of Analipsis hill is dominated by the Mon Repos estate (page 12).

Benitses ★★★

A stroll through the old village is like venturing into a secret garden through a pretty maze of narrow alleys, lemon orchards and white-washed houses. This is reputedly the home of the oldest olive tree in Greece – an amazing 750 years old. Benitses seafront is a mass of bars and tavernas, just right for a lively evening out. The **Corfu Shell Museum** at Benitses is one of Europe's best museums dedicated to shells and

Vlacherena Monastery, with Pontikonisi (Mouse Island) behind

other treasures of the sea. The highlights include a cowrie shell from Mozambique, listed in the *Guinness Book of Records* as the most precious shell in the world. Exotic souvenirs and unusual shells for collectors are on sale (ⓐ North end of Benitses Harbour Square ⓣ 26610 72227 ⓛ Open 10.00–20.00 ⓘ Small admission charge).

Kanoni ★★★

The Kanoni peninsula has probably the most famous and photographed view on Corfu, overlooking the two little islands of Pontikonisi (Mouse Island) and Vlacherena. Alongside is the Royal Hotel café and snack bar, enjoying those superb views on one side, but with a bird's-eye view of the rather less sublime airport runway on the other. You can walk down the winding steps to the little harbour from the terrace and along the causeway to Vlacherena with its picturesque little monastery. From here, take a boat to Pontikonisi and admire the Byzantine chapel hidden beneath the cypress trees.

BEACHES

Perama has a pleasant shingle beach reached by steep steps leading down from the main road. The shingle beach at Benitses is south of the old village alongside the main road and has a good range of water sports on offer. Aghios Ioannis, 4 km (2½ miles) south, also has good water sports from its sandy beach. For a change of scenery head to the west of Corfu, to Aghios Gordios with its wide, pale terracotta sands (page 31).

RESTAURANTS & BARS

Alkinoos €€€ Enjoy some of the best views in Perama from the terraces of this classy restaurant. The chicken is chargrilled to perfection and delicious Roquefort, wine or mushroom sauces complement the succulent steaks. ⓐ On the north side of the main road, opposite Avra Pub ⓣ 26610 41848

Captain's Taverna € 'Captain' George's patter continues while he cooks and serves home-made Greek food at its best. Little touches

MOUSE ISLAND?
There are several theories as to why Pontikonisi is called Mouse Island, including that it was once home to a million of the creatures, that it refers to its shape, or that it is just mouse size – it's for you to decide!

such as grilled pitta bread with your *taramasalata* and *tzatziki* are most welcome, but leave room for your main course. The portions are very generous – gargantuan meals at less than gargantuan prices. A favourite for everyone and there's a safe playground for children too. ❸ Just after the viewpoint, Kanoni 🕿 26610 40502 🕐 Open all day

🍸 **Kanoni** €–€€ Sip a cool beer whilst you take in the panorama. There's a splendid view over Perama, Pontikonisi and the white monastery on the islet of Vlacherena. ❸ Near the Corfu Holiday Palace Hotel, overlooking the sea

🍴 **Nausicaa** €€ Excellent, very popular restaurant serving Greek and international dishes and delicious puddings, from chocolate mousse to Greek *baklavas*. ❸ 11 Nafsikas, Kanoni, opposite Divani Hotel 🕿 26610 23492 🕐 Open for dinner

🍴 **Taverna S Sofia** €€ Live music accompanies friendly service at this upmarket Italian restaurant and piano bar with a large terrace overlooking the sea. If you've overdosed on *retsina*, rich red Italian wines flow freely here. ❸ Northern side of the main street going south 🕿 26610 21145 🕐 Open for lunch and dinner

NIGHTLIFE
If you're feeling lucky, spend an evening at the casino in the **Corfu Holiday Palace Hotel** (€€€ ❸ 2 Nafsikas, Kanoni 🕿 26610 46941 🕐 Open 20.00–03.00). There's a strict dress code, and don't forget your passport!

Moraitika & Messonghi
fun-lover's paradise and village character

Moraitika and Messonghi share the same long sweep of fine grey sand and shingle beach. Moraitika is larger and livelier, with plenty of restaurants and bars along the coastal road leading south to Messonghi. For a peaceful lunchtime or romantic evening, the old village up on the hillside has a couple of traditional tavernas in the maze of cobbled streets and whitewashed, flower-hung houses.

THINGS TO SEE & DO
Boat trip ★★
Messonghi Cruises run trips to Corfu Town, around the north-east coast and to the Blue Lagoon. **Zorba** runs trips to the salt mines in southern Corfu – find him on his boat at the mouth of the river between 17.30 and 21.30.

Cycling ★
Rent a bike from **Sammy's Bike Company** and cycle over to the unspoiled beaches by Lake Korission. ❸ Moraitika

Tennis ★
Have a game of tennis at the **Messonghi Beach Hotel**. ❸ Between Moraitika and Messonghi ❶ 26610 76684 ❷ Courts open 06.00–21.00

Water sports and scuba diving ★★
Learn to windsurf or sail a catamaran at **Wassersportstation** on the beach. You can also rent canoes and pedalos (❸ Moraitika ❶ 26610 75226). Or learn to scuba dive at the **Nautilus Diving School** . Run by a friendly Anglo-Greek couple, it's a recognized British Sub Aqua Club (BSAC) school. Trips for qualified divers are also organized and equipment hire is available (❸ In the grounds of the Messonghi Beach Hotel, between Moraitika and Messonghi ❶ 26610 83045 ❿ www.nautilusdivingcorfu.com ❷ Open May–Oct).

RESTAURANTS & BARS

 24 Hours € Good fast food, ice cream, coffee, snacks and main dishes. ⓐ Moraitika ⓛ Open all day

Bella Vista Taverna €€ It's a bit of a hike up the hill, but the views over the coast make it worthwhile. ⓐ In the old village, Moraitika ⓣ 26610 75460

Boukari Beach Restaurant €€ One of the best fish restaurants around. ⓐ Along the coast road to the south, in Boukari ⓣ 26610 51791

Memories € – €€ Charming Michales provides polite, professional service while his mother and brother conjure up Corfiot wonders in the kitchen. Lovely views of fishing boats from the smart terrace. ⓐ Messonghi ⓣ 26610 75607 ⓛ Open noon–16.00 and 19.00 onwards

Romantika € For a small admission fee you get a free drink and you can chill out all day long by the pool. Mid-week there's a barbecue with Greek dancing and plate smashing. ⓐ Moraitika ⓣ 26610 75238

Rose Garden €€ Set back from the road in an attractive shady, very romantic garden. The *mezedes* here are something special – sixteen different dishes of fried vegetables, dips and seafood. ⓐ Moraitika ⓣ 26610 75622 ⓛ Open 18.00–midnight

Sea Breeze € Family-run, very Greek taverna, right on the beach. ⓐ Messonghi ⓣ 26610 75284

Spiros Karidis €€ This taverna serves only fresh fish and sea-food. For something special, try the lobster. ⓐ A few kilometres from Messonghi (Boukari area) ⓛ Open daily

Village Taverna €€ The vine-covered terrace, with its geraniums and hydrangeas, is a lovely setting for sampling the Greek specialities. ⓐ In the old village, Moraitika

Village Taverna Marilena €€ One of the oldest restaurants in Messonghi, with a lively atmosphere. Children are warmly welcomed and carnivores will be more than happy with the seven-meat mixed grill. ⓐ Messonghi ⓣ 26610 75671

Whistles Beach Bar € Right on the beach – excellent value pizzas and snacks. ⓐ Messonghi, just along from Spyros on the beach

Zaks €€ Upmarket and professional, the speciality to seek out is the 'drunk man's stew', a dish traditionally made to use up whatever was in the fridge – a tasty concoction of pork or beef with peppers, chunks of cheese and sausages in a spicy sauce. ⓐ Messonghi ⓣ 26610 76036 ⓛ Open from 19.00

NIGHTLIFE

After Dark Try exotic cocktails and listen to international music from top DJs. ⓐ Moraitika ⓛ Open 19.00–02.00

Byblos Relax drinking your coffee at this friendly music café. ⓐ Moraitika ⓛ Open from noon onwards

Cadillac Club Bop until you drop. Look for the pink Cadillac bursting through the front wall. ⓐ Moraitika ⓛ Open from 22.00 onwards

Captain Morgan's An English DJ keeps feet a-thumping and bodies a-jumping. ⓐ Moraitika ⓘ Happy hour is 20.00–23.00

Golden Beach This gaudy pink bar on the beach has a Greek dancing display every evening and enough room for the kids to run around without upsetting anyone's beer. ⓐ Moraitika ⓛ Open 17.00–04.00

SHOPPING

MORAITIKA

3K's Shopping Centre A one-stop shop selling a wide range of toiletries, drinks and food. ☎ 26610 76220

Diesel Designer jackets, T-shirts, jeans, dresses and accessories at bargain prices.

Efi's Leather Market As well as the usual selection of handbags, belts and wallets, Efi's shop also has a variety of soft leather coats and jackets, shoes and slippers. ☎ 26610 75911

Fontana general market and souvenir shop In amongst the plastic lemons and plates decorated with furry dogs under glass, there are some pretty goblets, good-quality mugs, terracotta ceramics, leather gloves and some of the best postcards in the area. ☎ 26610 75281

MESSONGHI

Handmade Ceramics shop This little shop has a fine array of bright and pastel ceramics, many of which are copies of ancient Greek statues and pottery.

Natural Bakery A mouth-watering array of sticky *baklava*, doughnuts, cream cakes, *tiramisu* and a myriad of temptations for the sweet-toothed.

Shops in a Shop All your holiday needs are catered for under one big and airy roof. Clothes, including traditional hand-made Greek woollen slippers, jewellery, water sports equipment such as masks and snorkels, souvenirs, leather bags, as well as groceries, English newspapers and alcohol.

Very CoCo Friendly club with pool tables, big-screen TVs, live DJs, free entry and fast food. ➌ Moraitika ☎ 26610 75122 🕐 Open 24 hours, seven days a week

Kavos
discos, bars and beach

Stroll along Kavos' main street in the early evening and you could be in a ghost town. Do the same thing at 3 o'clock in the morning and you'll feel like you've landed on another planet. Disco competes with house music and neon signs flash gaudily.

Bars are loud and full of cocktails with suggestive names – everything in Kavos is 'screaming' or 'multiple'. It's geared to the party market ... it's brash, it's wild but it's also a huge amount of fun and one thing is for sure – you won't ever be bored.

On the northern fringes of Kavos, **St Peter's** is a quieter option, but still within easy reach of the action. There are water sports here too and a go-kart track and several beachside snack bars. Here you will find traditional Greek tavernas that also do great English breakfasts, pizza and pasta. Look out for all-inclusive menus which provide good value.

THINGS TO SEE & DO
Bungee jumping ★
Strictly for the fearless – or fuelled up! Choose from the bungee jump crane or rocket – or watch it all in comfort from the **British Restaurant** for a bird's-eye view.

Water sports ★★
Owing to its very sheltered position, this is a great place for water sports. Try parasailing or scuba diving in the clear waters or go fast and furious in the *Crazy Speedboat*.

BEACHES
Kavos beach is sandy, over 2 km (1½ miles) long, and shelves gently into the sea – the perfect place to gather your strength on the sandy beach whilst you plan the next evening's entertainment.

If you can tear yourself away from the bars and beach, a 30-minute (fairly energetic) walk south takes you to the crumbling monastery of **Arkoudillas** and the cliffs of **Cape Asporkavos**. Worth it for the superb coastal views across to the tiny island of **Paxos**. A boat trip from Kavos around Paxos is another option.

RESTAURANTS & BARS

All the restaurants, cafés and bars listed here are located on the main street in Kavos.

The Barn € This fast food place, part of the Barn complex, is usually at its busiest when clubbers in the grip of post-cocktail munchies come for a quick, cheap fix of hot dogs, burgers, chips or kebabs.

The British Restaurant € English food in large portions, served by friendly Greek waiters who break into a Greek dancing and plate-smashing routine most nights. Eat on the patio for a front-row view of the mad fools bungee jumping from the top of the crane opposite. ☎ 26620 61488

The Face € This spacious bar with large comfy chairs, pool tables and a huge video screen showing latest-release films throughout the day is perfect for vegging out and recovering from the night before.

Pizza Garden € The pizzas are enormous but don't worry if you can't eat it all, they'll box it up so you can take the rest home. ☎ 26620 61064

Uncle Harry's €–€€ Basic but tasty Greek and English food served on a large open veranda. Make a date for the Sunday lunch with all the trimmings. ☎ 26620 61442

NIGHTLIFE

Futures From midnight to the early hours, a mixture of tourists and locals dance and drink to house and rave music. It's the largest club in Kavos and top DJs from Ibiza take their turn at spinning the discs several times a summer.

JC's Drink flows freely – or at least cheaply – at JC's cocktail bar, particularly if you're mad enough to rise to the dentist's chair challenge. Take your position in the hot seat behind the bar and say 'Aaargh' whilst staff systematically pour throat-burning alcohol straight out of the bottle and into your mouth.

Rockys Always busy, this open-air bar buzzes with a party atmosphere, fuelled by the 'buy one, get one free' happy hour early on in the evening. Around 01.00, the doors close and English DJs play a mix of dance music to keep holidaymakers bopping till the early hours.

🔽 *Experience tranquillity on Kavos beach*

Aghios Georgios (south-west)
golden sands and water sports

This is part of the long, sandy stretch that fringes the whole south-west coastline of Corfu, framed by a backdrop of pine woods and olive trees, where you'll see the sign, 'Welcome to Corfu's best sandy beaches'. To the north of the resort are sand dunes and the saltwater lagoon, Nearby Lake Korission is a haven for wildlife, especially in the spring and autumn when it teems with migratory birds.

In Aghios Georgios itself, the more developed golden beaches have excellent water sports, perfect for all the family, and a good choice of tavernas overlooking the beach. There's a great selection of bars with quizzes, videos, bingo and karaoke, plus music and pool bars that buzz well into the small hours. Just inland is the traditional old Corfiot village of **Argirades**, worth a visit to see the lovely Venetian architecture and old monastery, or perhaps just to watch people and donkeys from a shaded café. Or, if you can tear yourself away from the golden sands and venture farther afield, **Corfu Town** is just 35 km (22 miles) north, with a regular bus service to get you there, departing twice daily.

Over 120 species of birds have been recorded as visitors to **Lake Korission** – especially during the winter months. But one all-seasons visitor is the mosquito: they are not malarial, but a pest none the less! Best defence is to cover up and apply plenty of good insect repellent.

THINGS TO SEE & DO
Boat trips ★
Kostas Boats has a regular service to the island of Paxos, four times weekly.
ⓐ In the centre of the main beach

Water sports ★★
Learn to parasail or water-ski: there are all sorts of activities available

here. **Nikos Sea Sports** is on the little port side of the beach. **Kosta's Jet Ski** is at the northern end of the beach, as is **Nautilus Diving**, a British Sub Aqua Club School with diving courses.

BEACHES

The most developed 'golden beach', offering a good range of water sports is at the southern end. There is a quiet beach a few minutes' walk north at Issos. The dunes north of here are the unofficial naturist area.

SHOPPING

Dolphin Gift Shop This shop sells high-quality ceramics and museum copies which are created by artist Katerina, whose special passion is dolphins – the symbol of good luck in Greece. She also specializes in porcelain, wind chimes and exquisitely crafted pieces in silver and gold. ❸ Next door to Zack's, near the port ❶ 26620 52852

RESTAURANTS & BARS

Dario's €–€€ The sunny yellow interior is matched by the cheerful waiters in this good Italian restaurant and beach bar which specialises in pizzas, spaghetti and crêpes. The terrace overlooks the beach and sea – making it the perfect place to watch the beautiful sunsets over a long, cool drink. ❸ Between the church and bus stop ❶ 26620 51555 ◑ Open evenings only

Kafesas €€ Atmospheric taverna, draped with fishing nets, specializing in traditional Corfiot dishes. The hospitable owner, Akis, and his New Zealand wife, Miriam, have three fishing boats working non-stop to supply them with the freshest fish, lobster, crab

◀ *Enjoy the golden sands of Aghios Georgios beach*

and mussels. You are positively encouraged to visit the kitchen to see what's cooking. With at least 100 different *mezedes* to choose from, you're spoilt for choice! ⓐ Near to the Golden Sands Hotel ⓣ 26620 51196 ⓛ Open all day ⓘ Saturday is Greek dancing night – reservations necessary

Panorama Bar €–€€ This aptly named bar also enjoys a perfect sea-edge location. On a clear day you can see as far south as the island of Paxos. ⓐ Next to Reflections Disco

San Carlos €–€€ Serving everything from breakfast to main dishes, this garden restaurant offers live music daily. ⓐ On the beach ⓛ Open all day

Zack's €–€€ Paradise for the sweet-toothed, with delicious creamy cappuccinos, mouth-watering pastries and home-made ice creams. As a bonus, there's also a special play area for children. ⓐ On the northern end of the beach, next to the Dolphin Gift Shop ⓣ 26620 52418

NIGHTLIFE

Café Bar Satellite TV and free pool are a popular combination here – and it gets quite lively. ⓐ Opposite the Golden Sands Hotel and St George's supermarket

Easy Busy Pub Lively atmosphere in this home from home – good value too. ⓐ Next to Lagoudias, near the Medical Centre

Malibu Mix of bar, café and taverna overlooking the beach. ⓐ Next to the water sports centres

Reflections Disco/Bar Good sounds in beautifully located beachside bar with great atmosphere. ⓐ Next to Panorama Bar

Traxx Very popular bar with football on the big screen, quiz and karaoke nights. ⓐ Next to Golden Sands Hotel

Aghios Gordios
spectacular scenery

At Aghios Gordios you will find one of the island's most beautiful beaches, with fascinating rock formations and sheer cliffs plunging into the sea. Headlands, hills, silvery olive groves and sandy stretches of soft golden sand with patches of shingle frame the crystal-clear blue waters.

Dominating the bay off the southern headland is a gigantic rock which resembles a tusk, called the **Ortholith**. At the northern end are **Plitri Point** and the rocky pinnacles of **Aerostatos** – formerly known as 'The Sentry' to keep a look-out for invaders and pirates. Whilst bathing here is very safe and the resort has one of the island's best beaches for children, the rocks at either end are excellent for snorkelling and spear-fishing and the resort is highly popular with water sports enthusiasts.

For a special treat, *astakos* (Greek for lobster) is hard to beat, but do check, because menus sometimes confuse the cheaper, saltwater crayfish with the king of the crustaceans. If in doubt, have a look at the claws: lobsters have a full set, crayfish are clawless – but both are delicious!

THINGS TO SEE & DO
Sinarades ★★
Just inland to the north of Aghios Gordios is this charming hill village, where winding streets lead past traditional old houses with flowers tumbling in bright profusion, to a lovely square with a fountain playing, shaded by tall palm trees – the meeting place for the locals (❶ A green bus goes from Aghios Gordios on the main road to Sinarades, or ask your holiday representative for further details).

Perhaps enjoy a coffee or long cool drink here before following the sign-posts up the alleyway to the excellent **Folk Museum of Central Corfu**, where you step back into a time-capsule of the 19th century, a Corfiot village house. It has a fine collection of local historical artefacts – and offers a rare glimpse into a vanishing way of life. Look out for the lovely shadow puppets on the second floor (ⓐ 2 Nikokavoura Street, Sinarades village ❶ 26610 54962 ● Open Mon–Sat 09.30–14.00, closed Sun ❶ Small admission charge).

Water sports ★

Try **Calypso Diving** to learn how to dive or practise your skills in the superb waters around here, perfect for diving (ⓐ 300 m (328 yd) on right from the Romantic Palace Restaurant ❶ 26610 53101). **Dimitri's** has facilities for a wide range of water sports (ⓐ On the beach in front of Sea Breeze Taverna).

RESTAURANTS & BARS

Alobar €€ This cosmopolitan café/cocktail bar in Aghios Gordios is named after a fictional character. As you are sipping away at your cocktail, you may catch sight of a famous model or singer. The best time to experience the atmosphere is at sunset. ⓐ A few metres away from the car park ● Open all day

The Mad Greek €€ Shaded by palm trees, this family-run and oriented restaurant has been going since 1994, serving steaks, fresh fish and Greek dishes. ⓐ Situated on a small street off the main road ❶ 26610 53743 ● Restaurant open daily from 18.00, bar open from noon

Romantic Palace Restaurant €€–€€€ Aptly named, a shady terrace overlooks the beach with superb cooking by owner-chef Michael Pangalis. Both he and his wife, Anna, ran restaurants

in Germany and have designed the restaurant and hotel beautifully.
There is a delicious range of traditional Greek and international dishes
on offer including fresh fish and lobster. Perfect for that special
occasion. ❸ Overlooking the beach ❶ 26610 53450
❶ Open all day

 Sea Breeze Taverna €€ All manner of Greek specialities,
barbecues and regular Greek nights and dancing make this
a very popular venue in an excellent location. There's even a playground
for the children. ❸ On the beach ❶ 26610 53214

 Taverna Sebastian €€ The oldest taverna in town, established in
1977. It does good home-made Greek and international food and
Corfiot specialities served on an atmospheric wide terrace. Special fish
nights and barbecues. Make sure you sample the good home-made
wines, in every colour, too. Does regular and spectacular Greek nights.
❸ Just off the main road ❶ 26610 53256

SHOPPING

Bakery Fresh bread brought from Sinarades and delicious
cakes and croissants are all on the menu here.
❸ Near to the church on the main road

Olive Wood Shop All kinds of bowls and carvings crafted in
luxuriant olive wood as well as a delightful selection of wind-
chimes. ❸ On the left-hand side, going up the main road
❶ 26610 53939

Venus Good-quality silver frames, icons and stylish modern
jewellery in this Aladdin's cave. ❸ Next door to the Olive
Wood Shop ❶ 26610 53939

Glyfada & Pelekas
superb sands & sunsets

Glyfada's long swathe of golden sands ranks amongst the best beaches on the island. The road down to the resort winds through olive groves to the bluest of shallow waters, sheltered by steep cliffs at either end. Several tavernas line the beach that is much sought-after for water sports as well as for swimming in the crystal-clear sea.

BEACHES

To the north lies **Myrtiotissa**, which was described by Lawrence Durrell in *Prospero's Cell* as 'perhaps the loveliest beach in the world', nowadays known (unofficially) as the island's naturist beach and a paradise for snorkellers. Best visited by boat, there are plenty of excursions and water-taxis from the surrounding area. Once there, you will find a beach bar and a tiny 14th-century monastery, dedicated to Our Lady of the Myrtles.

To the south of Glyfada is **Pelekas** whose long, sandy beach also attracts some naturists – but nowadays is best known for its excellent swimming and fabulous vantage points from the hilltop village inland. 'Kaiser's Lookout (Throne)' is the panoramic viewpoint much frequented by Kaiser Wilhelm II from his **Achilleion Palace** (page 86). This was his favourite spot on the island and he built a special telescope tower here to see his beloved sunsets more intimately. There are shops, tavernas and cafés clustered around the village and an excellent, sandy beach, accessible by car down a narrow, winding road.

Under Greek law, all beaches are freely accessible to the public – there are no private beaches. Going topless is now legal on most popular beaches, but nudism, whilst tolerated in designated areas, is still technically illegal so be careful where you take your clothes off.

● *The golden sands of Glyfada beach*

WATER SPORTS

Every manner of water sport is available from the beaches at Glyfada and Pelekas, among them parasailing, water-skiing, windsurfing and sailing. **Thomas's Water Sports** run water-skiing, parasailing and other activities. They also rent out motor boats by the hour so you can explore the neighbouring beaches – or use their taxi boat service from Pelekas beach.

For a special treat take a full-day boat trip from Glyfada in a trimaran, all-inclusive of lunch and drinks, or indulge in a moonlit romantic trip (pricey but worth it). Ask your holiday representative for more details.

RESTAURANTS & BARS

Agnes Café Bar & Restaurant €–€€ Feast on fresh sardines, Corfiot specialities like *pastitsada* and delicious beef *sofrito* or snack on Greek salads laden with feta cheese. ⓐ Glyfada, on the beach ⓣ 26610 94231 ⓛ Open for lunch and dinner

Aloha Beach Bar €–€€ Breakfast, lunch and delicious *mezedes* in the evening with wine from the barrel. Latin American and reggae music, with dancing from around 17.00 until late. ⓐ Glyfada, in the middle of the beach ⓣ 26610 94380 ⓛ Open all day

Banana Club €€ Great atmosphere in this hilltop setting with all kinds of music from jazz and ethnic to the sounds of today. ⓐ On Pelekas road to Kaiser's Lookout

Golden Beach Restaurant & Bar €–€€ A great beachside location, this taverna specializes in fresh fish but also serves snacks throughout the day. Try the delicious swordfish. ⓐ Glyfada, southern side of the beach near to the Louis Grand Hotel ⓣ 26610 94223 ⓛ Open for lunch and dinner

Gorgona €€ Delicious Greek specialities and fresh fish in a pleasant, friendly environment. ⓐ Glyfada, southern end of beach ⓣ 26610 94336 ⓛ Open for lunch and dinner

Jimmy's €–€€ Good authentic Greek family taverna. ⓐ Pelekas village ⓣ 26610 94284

 Louis Grand Hotel, Glyfada €€–€€€ This large, luxurious hotel, elegantly furnished with antiques, dominates Glyfada beach. It has several comfortable bars and restaurants and superb views across the sandy beach. The **Figareto Restaurant** serves good buffets – eat as much as you like for a fixed price on the panoramic terrace. Perfect for a special occasion. ⓐ Glyfada, southern end of beach ⓣ 26610 94140 ⓛ Open 18.30–21.30

Maria's Place €–€€ This family-run taverna dates back to the times when hippies used to crash out on the beach. Maria and Costa's son, Andreas, has a fishing boat and delivers his fresh catch daily – swordfish, red mullet, *kalamari* (squid), marlin and octopus regularly feature on the menu. There are great barbecues, delicious home-made wine, Greek dancing two or three times a week and fun-filled beach parties where you can dance the night away. ⓐ Pelekas beach ⓣ 26610 94601 ⓛ Open all day

Spiros Taverna €–€€ Fresh fish is the speciality here, overlooking the sea. Delicious squid and lobster and good value snacks served all day in high season. ⓐ Pelekas beach ⓣ 26610 94641

Sunset Restaurant €€–€€€ Lovely terrace with stunning views – especially at sunset. Part of the luxury Sunset Hotel with both Greek and international specialities to match. ⓐ Located high up by Kaiser's Lookout, about 3 km (2 miles) out of town ⓣ 26610 94230 ⓛ Open all day

Taverna Glyfada Beach €–€€ Family-run bar and taverna serving good Greek specialities and fish – look out for the catch of the day. Lovely setting right on the northern end of the beach. ⓐ Glyfada beach ⓣ 26610 94487 ⓛ Open for lunch and dinner

Ermones
lovely bay and legendary landing place

Picturesque little Ermones lies between two steep headlands, which tumble down from the fertile Ropa Valley. According to legend, Homer's Odysseus was washed ashore in a state of exhaustion after his ten-year voyage home from the Trojan Wars. He was found by the beautiful Nausicaa who had come to wash clothes with her handmaidens at a nearby stream – said to be that of Paleokastritsa or Ermones and its beach – according to mythology. He was given shelter and then eventually returned home to his native island of Ithaca.

The Ropa river flows out to the sea at Ermones, which has a fine shingle and sand beach and now flies an EU Blue Flag. The sea is beautifully clear, excellent for snorkelling, and there are numerous water sports on offer. There's also a safe rock pool for children – perfect for crabbing.

There are some good wines on Corfu and the rarest (and most expensive) bottled wine is Theotoki, a dry white produced from the local grapes of the Ropa Valley. Worth seeking out, perhaps as a change from the usual house wine out of a barrel.

THINGS TO SEE & DO
Golf ★★★
Corfu's only golf club, **The Corfu Golf and Country Club**, is just inland from Ermones in the Ropa Valley. This famous 18-hole course is 6 km (4 miles) long with a par of 72 and has been described as one of the greatest courses in Europe. It certainly has a few challenges with water hazards and a design making it more like a links course, and is very popular with golfers from all over the island. Clubs are available for hire and lessons with qualified pros: good shop, clubhouse with bar and restaurant at the 19th hole. ⓐ Ropa Valley ☏ 26610 94220 ❶ Book ahead

◗ *Ermones beach is excellent for swimming*

Horse riding ★★★

The Ropa Valley just above the beach at Ermones is one of the most beautiful and fertile areas of the island. Here you can ride amongst fig, pear and apple trees and through vine-yards which stretch for miles. Ponies and horses are available from **Ropa Valley Riding Stables** for both novice and experienced riders. Rides are for approximately two hours with a stop for refreshment.
🅐 On the approach road to Ermones ❶ 26610 94220

⬤ *The crystal-clear sea is ideal for diving*

Water sports ★★

Odyssey Divers offers fantastic scuba diving from the beach in crystal-clear waters which shelve quickly into the deep. 🅐 On the beach ❶ 26610 94241

EXCURSION
Aqualand ★★★

Get 'Wet 'n' Wild' at Aqualand which has to be one of the best water adventure parks in Europe. Ride the Kamikaze, plunge into the Black Hole, twirl around the Crazy River, relax in the Lazy River, then attempt the Slippery Frog, Hydrotube, Four Twisters, a quick whirl in the Big Jacuzzi – before starting all over again! There are also slides of all sizes, a games arcade, a 'wet and dry' bar, bouncing castle and children's pool. This is an excellent day out for all the family and the admission price – quite high – includes everything, from the rides and all facilities to the use of sunbeds and parasols around the pools. The well-stocked souvenir shop, boutique, bars, ice cream parlour and restaurants are, of course, extra. It's extremely popular and attracts visitors from all over the island. 🄰 Aqualand is at Aghios Ioannis on the Pelekas to Ermones road 🄸 26610 52963/58351 🄻 Open 10.00–18.00 (May–Oct); 10.00–19.00 (July and Aug)

RESTAURANTS & BARS

Dizzy's Music Café Bar € Music from the 1960s, through Latin American and reggae right up to today's sounds, which makes for a great atmosphere and, as their slogan goes, some 'interesting nights'. 🄰 Next to the Sunmarotel Calimera Ermones Beach and Supermarket Ermones 🄻 Open evenings until late

George's Taverna €–€€ Fresh fish is the speciality here with lobster on request – best to reserve in advance. Or try the delicious *mezedes* – a meal in themselves. 🄸 26610 94506 🄻 Open all day

Maria's Taverna €–€€ Spiros makes you welcome here at this adjoining taverna to George's with the same beautiful views over the sea. The food's pretty good too! 🄸 26610 94659 🄻 Open all day

Sunmarotel Calimera Ermones Beach €€–€€€ This hotel, previously known as Ermones Beach Hotel, dominates the little bay of Ermones. A funicular railway runs down from the hotel to the beach, and a ride on this will take you to the good restaurant which serves Corfiot specialities and fresh seafood. 🄰 On the north side of the river overlooking the beach 🄸 26610 94241 🄻 Open for lunch and dinner

Taverna Nafsica (Nausicaa) €–€€ Brothers George and Nikos extend a warm welcome to this beachside taverna where good Corfiot specialities and delicious red mullet feature amongst the fresh fish on the menu. Greek dancing twice a week with live music (no extra charge). 🄰 Part of the Ermones Golf Hotel, on the south side of the river 🄸 26610 94236/94045 🄻 Open all day

Paleokastritsa & Liapades
picturesque bays

Picturesque Paleokastritsa sits above a craggy coastline below densely wooded hillsides. The sea is particularly refreshing here, as it's one of the coolest spots on the island. Nestling against a dramatic backdrop of cliffs, cypress trees and maquis-covered rocks, neighbouring Liapades has one of the most peaceful beaches on the island. It's the perfect place for snorkelling as the rocks drop directly down into the sea, acting as host to a wide variety of marine life.

THINGS TO SEE & DO
Angelokastro ★★★
Angelokastro, a ruined 13th-century fortress that stands on a rocky cliff near the village of Krini, was originally built to defend Corfu from pirate raids in Byzantine times. The views are unrivalled, with a 360-degree panorama over the craggy coastline and the Paleokastritsa monastery.

Boating/diving ★★★
Hire a motor boat or glass-bottomed boat and visit the caves and deserted beaches between Liapades and Ermones or try scuba diving with experienced divers from the **Corfu Diving Center**.

Lakones ★★★
Take the path (signposted to Lakones) to the left of the Odysseus Hotel. After about 45 minutes, you'll come out into the back alleyways of Lakones with its jumble of whitewashed houses. The **Café Olympia**, on the main road, is a good place for a drink. From here, head west along the coastal road to the Bella Vista for a wonderful panoramic view over the monastery (page 44) and the sparkling sapphire sea. You'll pass an olive wood workshop where you can see a local craftsman painstakingly shaping the wood.

◐ *Paleokastritsa is a perfect place for snorkelling*

Liapades ★★

Liapades has delightful old Venetian manor houses and courtyards, narrow twisting lanes and a lovely church. Wizened old men sit nodding sagely in the village square as women, riding side-saddle, trundle past on their donkeys after long mornings working in the vineyards.

Paleokastritsa monastery ★★★

Paleokastritsa monastery, located on a headland jutting out into the sea, is now home to a few monks. The small church (built in 1722) has a beautiful carved ceiling and the tiny museum has the skeleton of a 'sea monster' (actually a whale) found by the crew of a French ship in 1860.
🛈 26630 41210 🕒 Open daily 08.00–13.00 and 15.00–20.00

For women visiting the monastery, long trousers/skirts and covered shoulders are the order of the day, otherwise you'll be handed a fetching elasticated skirt and/or shawl at the door in return for a donation.

BEACHES

The white-pebbled **Aghia Triada beach** at the eastern end of the village is one of the largest, and is popular with families. The two neighbouring beaches, **Platakia** and **Alipa**, are rather quieter. Trendy young teenagers head for the sandy strip at **Aghios Spiridon**. The smaller **Aghios Petros** and **Ambelaki bays** lie on the western side of the peninsula. If you're in the area for more than one day, sail along the coast of Liapades and visit **Stelari beach**, which is accessible only by boat.

SHOPPING

Makrades, the next village after Lakones, has a plethora of handicraft shops offering olive wood, local wine, natural sponges, carpets, embroidered table linen, olive-oil soap and pure lambswool hand-made jumpers at bargain prices.

Take a reasonably priced, half-hour trip in a fishing boat from the main beach to visit the **Blue Eye Caves** (Caves of Nausicaa) – rumoured to be where Odysseus met Nausicaa in Homer's ancient Greek epic.

RESTAURANTS

Anemomylos €€ Enjoy an unrivalled view of the bay whilst you dine on the Greek and international specialities here. Check out the bouzouki night, usually Friday, when professional dancers, accordion players and violinists show off their skills – and you'll be given the opportunity to join in. ⓐ Entrance to old village of Liapades on the way up from the beach

Golden Fox €–€€ Built on the mountainside offering magnificent views of the sheltered bays of Paleokastritsa and the Ionian Sea. This family-run restaurant, part of a complex offering accommodation, a bar and swimming pool, offers delicious home-made food and pastries. ⓐ Just outside Lakones ⓣ 26630 49101 ⓛ Open all day

Michalis €–€€ A good selection of Greek specialities and international dishes are served at bargain prices. A four-course set-price menu will set you back you very little, and there is plenty of choice for children. ⓐ Entrance to old village of Liapades on the way up from the beach ⓣ 26630 41178

Poseidon Beach €€–€€€ By the sea, and an excellent, relaxing place to stop off after a visit to Paleokastritsa. Serves good local food and fish too. ⓐ Aghia Triada beach ⓣ 26630 41225 ⓛ Open daily, all day

Vrachos €€ Good family restaurant. Enjoy fresh fish while relaxing with a view of Paleokastritsa bay. ⓐ At the road junction, on the way to the monastery ⓣ 26630 41233 ⓛ Open 09.00–midnight

Aghios Georgios (north-west)
long sandy beach

The south-facing bay at Aghios Georgios stretches for over 3 km (nearly 2 miles) backed by statuesque cypress trees and olive groves. The beach has an EU Blue Flag, awarded for its pristine beach and clear sea, which is excellent for all kinds of water sports, especially for windsurfing.

THINGS TO SEE & DO
Walking ★
Take a walk around the bay to the quiet little village of Afionas, which sits on top of Cape Arillas, the northern part of Aghios Georgios bay. The path from the village square leads you down to a glorious panoramic outlook with views to the west towards the island of Kravia. From here you can follow the steepish footpath on to the cape and below there are two secluded little shingle beaches which are excellent for snorkelling.

Water sports ★★
Diving Fun Club The glorious scenery above the surface of the sea is matched by the natural beauty under the sea, waiting for you to discover. For beginners and experienced alike. ❶ 26630 96092

Sun Fun Club Water Sports Stakis and Helen cater for most water activities here on the beach from paragliding to hiring your own motorboat or taking water-taxis to the neighbouring beaches. ❶ 26630 96355

Windsurfing School This place offers tuition and boards for hire. ⓐ Opposite the Delfini Restaurant

RESTAURANTS & BARS
Akrogiali €€–€€€ Excellent fish restaurant down a track. Push the boat out with specialities such as lobster spaghetti, but

check the price first! *Bourdeto* (the local fish stew) is less expensive.
ⓐ At the south end of the beach – look out for the windmill
ⓣ 69773 34278 ⓛ Open daily for lunch and dinner

Anonymous Bar €–€€ This cocktail bar and restaurant is all in pink and the owners, Alex and Andronicus, make you very welcome. Specialities include home-made pizzas, moussaka and traditional Greek food. ⓐ Overlooking the beach ⓣ 26630 96339 ⓛ Open all day

Delfini €€ Big terrace overlooking the sea with a bird's-eye view of the windsurfing school (page 46), serving breakfasts, snacks, pizzas and excellent *mezedes* as well as fresh fish. ⓐ By the beach
ⓣ 26630 96323 ⓛ Open all day until late

Fisherman €€ Long-established local favourite which doesn't have a phone or even electricity! It specializes in fish of all kinds, including Corfiot specialities. One of its unusual dishes is prawns cooked in *ouzo*. Delicious – especially when seated outdoors, around the enormous olive tree in the middle of the small garden. ⓐ Set in the olive groves (look for the sign) ⓛ Open daily for lunch and dinner

Vrachos €€ The best place for lobster and crayfish, which are on the menu every day. You're guaranteed a warm welcome from the owner, Costas, on his beachside restaurant terrace, as well as gorgeous views across the bay. Also serves Corfiot specialities such as *sofrito*, all manner of fresh fish, and good hamburgers. ⓐ On the beach
ⓣ 26630 96373 ⓛ Open all day

NIGHTLIFE
Balloon Club Aghios Georgios's disco has good dance music from the 1960s right up to the second millennium, played by lively DJs. The action starts winding up around 23.30 until the small hours. ⓐ After the bridge going out of town ⓛ Open Fri–Sun

Arillas
safe sandy bathing

The mainly sandy, Blue Flag beach shelves very gently into the shallow turquoise sea, making this an ideal spot for families. Lying at the northern end of a long bay, the setting is spectacular with a lovely backdrop of green hills and olive groves, and excellent views of the little island of Kravia (known as 'Ship Island') to the south.

THINGS TO SEE & DO
Water sports ★★
Arillas Water Sports Parasailing, water-skiing, windsurfers, pedalos and canoes are all available for hire here. ⓐ Kiosk on the beach

Flamingo's This is a free freshwater swimming pool – relax with a drink beside the pool. There is also a happy hour. ⓐ Next to Porto Fino taverna on the beach

RESTAURANTS
Arillas Inn €€ Relax under Takis' vine-covered terrace and enjoy a long cool drink – perhaps an iced coffee or feast on lobster, steaks or mezedes. There's also Greek dancing and plate smashing every Wednesday. ⓐ By the sea ⓣ 26630 51070 ⓛ Open all day

Marina Restaurant €€ Right on the seafront, this shaded terrace has a warm, welcoming atmosphere and serves Greek specialities, fresh fish and delicious grilled lobster. ⓐ Part of the Marina Hotel on the seafront ⓣ 26630 51102 ⓛ Open all day

SHOPPING
Ina's Tourist and Gift Shop Sells 'designer' T-shirts, wraps and sarongs, all at good prices. ⓐ Next to Cavia Supermarket

🔺 *Water-skiing along the bay at Arillas can make for a memorable day*

🍴 **Porto Fino** €–€€ Spiro and Helen will serve you a full English breakfast in this beachside taverna as well as steaks and good home-cooked Greek dishes. ⓐ Next door to Arillas Inn ⓣ 26630 51834 🕐 Open all day

🍴 **Restaurant Graziella** € A large restaurant extends out on to the terrace looking across the sea where Aris, the owner, assures you of a warm welcome. Good-value inclusive menus, and fresh fish is the speciality. ⓐ Seafront ⓣ 26630 51039 🕐 Open for lunch and dinner

🍴 **Thalassa** €€ Overlooking the sea, this lovely taverna serves traditional home-made Greek dishes, good fresh fish – and you can choose your own live lobster! There's also a children's menu available. ⓐ On the seafront 🕐 Open all day ⓘ Greek dancing every Monday at 21.00 at no extra charge

NIGHTLIFE

Coconut Bar Serves over 100 exotic cocktails as English DJs play the best sounds of this (and the last) century. ⓐ Main street running down to the beach ⓣ 26630 51150 🕐 Open until very late

Malibu Sky sports, karaoke and English DJ in this atmospheric air-conditioned nightclub which buzzes until very late. ⓐ Next to Coconut Bar, on the main street ⓣ 26630 51243

Aghios Stefanos
popular family resort

A wide stretch of sand sweeps round a sparkling bay enclosed on one side by cliffs and on the other by the red-roofed village nestling on the hills. Best of all, it's relatively undiscovered – little danger here of someone reading over your shoulder! The resort is a haven for seekers of tranquility – there is nothing more restful than watching the fishing boats return in the afternoon. However, despite being so low-key, there are plenty of quality tavernas and a couple of venues where the dancing continues until the small hours.

THINGS TO SEE & DO
Arillas ★
Walk to the village of Arillas (page 48) for lunch or dinner at one of the seaside tavernas (as for the chapel – see opposite – but turn left at the top). The stroll there is flower-strewn, fragrant and filled with birds and butterflies, while crickets sing in the undergrowth. The panorama over the bay at San Stefanos and the narrow beach at Arillas is stunning. Paths are rough and uneven – flat shoes are a good idea.

Boating ★★
Take a sunbathing, sightseeing and swimming boat trip to the attractive Diapontia islands – Mathraki, Othoni and Ereikoussa – off the north-western coast. Nearhos does daily boat trips in summer.

Parasailing ★★
Go parasailing with a friend – tandem rides will save you money on individual prices. ⓐ Look for Captain Niko's kiosk on the beach

Tennis ★
Courts are available for rent near the Perros apartments, with lessons for beginners. Go to the house opposite the courts, no. 168, for information.

SHOPPING

 Perdita's Glass Art A fabulous shop selling which sells stunning original hand-made glass items and jewellery.
☎ 26630 51384

Walking ★
Take a walk up to the 18th-century Aghios Stefanos chapel at the southernmost point of the bay. You can either follow the track alongside the Hotel Nafsica's pool or, for a gentler climb, take the path opposite the **Summer Dream restaurant**. The walk up affords lovely views over the beach and hills beyond. Try to make the trip towards the end of the day when the wild thyme and jasmine perfumes of the Mediterranean *maquis* are at their strongest.

RESTAURANTS
There are no road names in Aghios Stefanos; the main road to Arillas has all the restaurants, cafés and bars listed here except for the **Athens Bar** and the **Condor Club**, which are on the road running north.

Barras Bar €€ One of the oldest restaurants in the resort, it's well equipped for families, with slides, free use of the pool and sun-loungers. ☎ 26630 51047 ⏰ Open all day

O Manthos Taverna €€ A warm welcome awaits you on this airy veranda overlooking the beach. The menu is traditional Greek, with simple dishes for children, and specialities include tender chargrilled chicken, and barbecued braised beef. Saturday night is Greek dancing night. ☎ 26630 52197 ⏰ Open for lunch and dinner

Mistral €€ The tempting aroma of barbecued meat mingles with the sea breeze on Mistral's beachside patio. ☎ 26630 52072

Nafsica €€ Service is professional and polite and the menu is peppered with unusual dishes as well as Greek and international staples. Set your taste buds tingling with the Nafsica special – a tasty melting pot of bacon, cheese and mushrooms served on the pleasant and shaded terrace with a view down to the sea. Varied and tasty range for vegetarians. 🕿 26630 51051 🕒 Open all day

Sunset Taverna €€ This is a family-oriented restaurant with fun Greek nights every Saturday, more often in high season. Sample the popular speciality, lamb *stamna*, on the rose-filled terrace or enjoy the lovely views up into the hills over a dinner of delicately grilled red snapper or swordfish. 🕿 26630 51185

Zorba's €€€ Ancient Greek specialities, ranging from prawns in apricot sauce with beetroot and artichokes, through to sausages and lentils with garlic and rosemary, are served in a wonderful setting that promises an unforgettable dining experience. 🕿 69377 35595

NIGHTLIFE

Athens Bar Go with the flow at this wacky and fun bar. The staff are always joking and full of life and the music reflects the mood of the clientele, sometimes rocking to reggae, at others, dancing wildly to house. 🕿 26630 51764

Condor Club A varied crowd gathers in the large front bar for dinner and cocktails, quizzes and bingo. At midnight, locals and holidaymakers, young and old, head to the spacious club at the back to bop the night away to international music. 🕿 26630 95438

Magnet Bar Shows movies and has karaoke nights and dancing.

Sundowner Bar British-owned establishment which has regular live entertainment and sport on TV.

Sidari
lazy days, vibrant nights

Days spent in Sidari are sleepy and languid, with nothing more demanding than lazing on the beach, paddling about on a pedalo or sitting in the shade of one of the many beach bars. Come the evening, the atmosphere fast-forwards to vibrant and lively. The hardest choice you'll have to make, though, is which restaurant to choose and whether to take to the stage in a karaoke performance or simply dance until dawn.

THINGS TO SEE & DO
By bike or horse ★

Hire a mountain bike for the day and go as you please. The truly energetic can take a 12 km (7½ miles) guided cycle tour through quiet country lanes and olive groves. Alternatively, let the horse take the strain whilst you enjoy the scenery. Visit **Mountain Mania**, or the **Yellow Boat Company** office (❶ 26630 95555).

Go-karting ★★

Hit the tracks at **Sidari Go-Karts**, near the BP garage. Adults can choose low or high-powered karts according to their kamikaze tendencies and ability. Mini karts are available for kids under five.

Water sports ★★

Explore the northern coastline in a motorboat. Contact the **Yellow Boat Company**, on the beach or at the office, and ask for Paula or George. ❶ 26630 95555 ❶ No permit required

Spend a day at **Sidari Water Slide**. The kids will love splashing about in the pool and on the slides. Tickets are inexpensive, sunbeds and umbrellas free. There's a snack bar serving sandwiches, spaghetti and drinks. ❷ The water-slide is behind the 'Value Plus' office and is clearly signposted throughout the resort ❶ 26630 99066

BEACHES

Sidari beach stretches the entire length of the main road, a long sweep of dark terracotta sand lapped by warm, shallow water. At the western end of the beach in the Canal d'Amour area are several sandy coves enclosed by rocky gorges. **Sunset Beach**, a few kilometres west of Sidari, is one of the best spots in Corfu to watch the sun go down. The setting is spectacular – a narrow strip of sand set at the bottom of sheer cliffs.

Local legend claims that swimming in the Canal d'Amour guarantees a lifetime of love with your dream partner.

RESTAURANTS

 Bolero € Large portions of English food and a few Corfiot specialities are served in this pub-cum-garden bar with interesting choices for vegetarians and kids. Come 22.00, the decades roll back to the 1960s and 1970s and would-be pop stars sing their hearts out in the nightly karaoke sessions. ⓐ Main street ❶ 26630 95244 🕒 Open all day

 Captain's €€ Serving fresh fish as well as pasta or steaks. Look out for the big fish-shaped sign. ⓐ Main street

Elysee €€ The owner, Takis, gives you a warm welcome to his family restaurant, which serves breakfast, snacks, main dishes, ice cream. ⓐ On the beach front 🕒 Open 09.00–02.00

Hawaii €€ Greek home cooking, fresh fish and mouth-watering ice creams in this grillroom bar. ⓐ Opposite the Amadeus Bar, Main street ❶ 26630 95195

Hong Kong Palace €€ This clean and tasteful Chinese restaurant makes a welcome alternative from moussaka, or you can opt for a take-away for a quiet night in. ⓐ Main street 🕒 Open for dinner only

The long stretch of Sidari beach has beautiful dark terracotta sand

Margarita €€ Steaks – fillet, peppered, with lobster – are on the menu and jolly good they are too. If you've gone native, the *kokinisto*, *sofrito* and *stifado* are prepared to perfection. ❸ Main street

Olympic €€–€€€ Dine on the lovely rear terrace at Sidari's oldest taverna, under a canopy of jasmine flowers. If you like to people-watch, the seating at the front overlooks the main street. ❸ Next to Bolero ❶ 26630 95945

Pizza Romana €€ Fresh pizzas, home-made chilli and *souvlaki*. Live Greek music Saturday nights. ❸ Kahlua pool, Canal d'Amour

Tequila Tex-Mex Bar and Grill €€ Homemade authentic Tex-Mex food, prepared fresh every day. Also has the best vegetarian and vegan menu in Sidari. Sociable bar open beyond restaurant hours, to around 03.00, serving imported Mexican tequilas, mezcals and cocktails to a background of latin/jazz/motown/soft rock music. ❶ 26630 99335

 The little village square has an umbrella of huge plane trees, the Greek symbol of stability and protection. A good place to enjoy a cool drink and discuss politics and philosophy – or just a good old gossip – as centuries of Greeks have done.

SHOPPING

The Pottery Shop A large selection of ceramics, including original museum copies. ❸ On the main street

Tassos and Bill A reasonable selection of belts, wallets and bags, but the real bargains are the fur-lined slippers, in the softest suede, and the leather gloves.

Wood and Stone A good stop for inexpensive presents. Wooden toys, hairclips and smooth shiny quartz are budget buys, with plenty of olive-wood bowls, pots and vases if you're feeling flush.

NIGHTLIFE

Arena Bar During the day it's a beach bar, big on baked potatoes, chip butties and ice creams. At night, the emphasis shifts to cocktails and karaoke with a happy hour from 19.00 to 21.00 to give you the courage you need.

Faros A restaurant and beach bar during the day, Faros transforms into a dance bar by night with a great fun atmosphere and every disco classic since the 1960s played by English DJs. Also featuring cabaret acts from the UK and karaoke spots. There's seating upstairs for a quieter drink and a bird's-eye view of gyrating bodies. ❶ 26630 95012
❶ Admission charge after 23.00, but look out for free-entry fliers handed out on the beach

Remezzo's In early and late season, Remezzo's opens nightly for a non-stop mixture of dance and pop music. Entry is often free for the ladies – sorry, lads. Rumoured to have foam parties too! At the height of the season, the action moves to the larger sister club, **Caesar's**, which holds 1500 merrymakers, compared with Remezzo's 500. Dance music blasts out from 23.00 till dawn, with the option of drinking under the stars in the fountain-filled garden bar. ❶ Admission charge for both

Scorpion Bar Popular with Brits as it regularly shows the TV soaps from back home, and gets very lively later.

Theo and Billy's Cocktail Bar All ages can enjoy the lively atmosphere of this entertaining pub. There's bingo, pool, video games, satellite and Sky TV, or you can just relax over a cocktail whilst the DJ plays jazz, blues and up-to-date dance music at a level that allows you to talk to your friends without the help of a megaphone.

Venus Guinness sign outside welcomes you to a wide selection of beers, subdued lighting and pre-1985 music, making this a popular watering hole for the over-30s. ❶ 26630 95961

Roda
beaches and nightlife

Once a quiet fishing village, Roda has become a favourite with families who love the long sand-and-pebble beach and safe shallow water. There are plenty of pretty walks, water sports, pony treks and excursions available for those who start to fidget after a few days of doing nothing.

THINGS TO SEE & DO
Kassiopi ★★
Drive or take a bike ride towards Kassiopi. The coastal road is really spectacular, fringed with lush olive trees on one side, jagged rocks jutting into a sparkling sea on the other and the coast of Albania looming in the distance.

Horse riding and walking ★★
Go pony trekking along country lanes, through the olive groves, down to Agnos beach. Take a stroll into the hills towards the little Greek villages of Sfakera, Platanos and Nymphes – step back in time along the cobbled alleyways amongst old stone houses or walk along the beach to Almyros (unless you're easily embarrassed – this is a nudist 'hangout').

RESTAURANTS

 Bootleggers € Friendly restaurant serving the best pizzas in town. ⓐ On the main street ⓣ 26630 63435

 Drosia €€ Traditional taverna serving enormous chargrilled steaks and garlicky *tzatziki* served as the Greeks originally intended before British supermarkets got in on the act. ⓐ On the main street

 Enigma €–€€ Serves Greek, Chinese, Indian, Mexican, British and American specialities, this restaurant caters for all tastes. The children's menu and spacious terrace make it a good choice for families

looking for a night out. ➋ On the main street, just past Drunken Sailor
➊ 69761 16246

Golden Sand €€ Food served all day and Greek dancing every
night. ➌ On the sea front

New Port €€ Gentle jazz and a sea view with standard Greek
and international fare. ➌ On the front

Odysseus €–€€ Menu offers many different starters and good
grilled food. ➌ On main street ➊ 26630 63459 ➍ Open all day

Pancalos €–€€ Spit-and-sawdust taverna housed in the oldest
building in Roda, with simple tables on a balcony overlooking the
sea and the freshest of fish – indulge in sole, lobster or giant prawns.
➌ On the sea front

Roda Inn Village Restaurant €€ Look for this hotel by the sea
and sample its restaurant, which is good and open to non-
residents. There is Greek music too. ➊ 26630 63358 ➍ Open daily
for lunch and dinner

Roda Park €€ Traditional Greek cuisine, including *bekhri
mezedes*, a mouth-watering combination of pork, ham, cheese,
mushrooms cooked in wine sauce and *gioylbassi*, tender chicken baked in
a parcel with potatoes. ➌ The old village ➊ 26630 63212 ➍ Open all day

Spiros No 1 €–€€ Home-cooked Greek dishes, a spotlessly clean
pool, free sunbeds, quiz and bingo nights, pool parties and, best of
all, Spiros' potent trio of special cocktails. It's welcoming to children and
well worth the short walk out of town. Don't miss the legendary Greek
dancing night once a week – for the cost of a reasonably priced set
menu, you'll have ringside seats and lots of fun. ➌ Turn left at the end
of the main street ➊ 26630 63429 ➍ Open for lunch and dinner

NIGHTLIFE

Cheers II Always game for a laugh and a joke, outgoing Paula and her husband, Gary, offer a warm welcome to their friendly pub. ❸ Old village

The Drunken Sailor One of the liveliest clubs in Roda because of its soundproofing. When Greek law dictates that the music must be turned down, they simply shut the doors and hike up the volume for dancing till dawn. ❸ Main street

Maggie's Place British-run pub attracting a 30-plus crowd to its trivia quizzes, excellent bar meals and a relaxed background of 1960s music. Maggie also bakes some mean scones, served with jam and cream, for an indulgent afternoon tea. ❸ Main street ❻ 26630 64516

Mistral Snacks and film shows during the day, cocktail bar in the evening, full-throttle dance bar by night. Don't miss the Greek dancing, which literally plays with fire! ❸ Main street ❻ 26630 64477

Roxanne's At 23.00 the action begins in this open-air beer garden opposite the Skouna Club, where revellers of all ages dance under the stars. ❶ Harbour ❹ Weekends only out of season

🔻 *Roda is a favourite with families*

Acharavi
peaceful beach resort

Acharavi is set along the main coastal road between Kassiopi and Roda, with hills to one side and a long wide sand-and-pebble beach to the other. A good base for exploring the northern coastline, it's also within reach of the island's highest point – the peak of Mount Pantokrator.

THINGS TO SEE & DO
Hydropolis ★★★
The second largest water park in Corfu has three pools: the Kamikaze, hydrotubes and jacuzzi. Listen to DJ music, play volleyball, basketball, tennis, water polo or have a coffee at the Internet café.

Mount Pantokrator ★★★
Head up to the peak of Mount Pantokrator for spectacular views over Corfu, Albania and the Greek mainland to the east. There's a tiny monastery on the peak (906 m/3000 ft) as well as less attractive telecommunication masts.

Old Perithia ★★
Eerie but fascinating, this old village, 700 m (about half a mile) up on the slopes of Mount Pantokrator, is almost completely deserted. Entire streets of Venetian houses now stand empty. For centuries, the area was densely populated because its inaccessible position kept the village safe from pirate raids. With the development of the coast, the population of Old Perithia gradually dwindled. Today, there are several friendly tavernas serving drinks and meals to curious tourists.

RESTAURANTS & BARS
Avra €€ Situated in a beautiful environment, this restaurant offers good quality food. The chef recommends spaghetti with seafood, lobster and local wine. There is also a playground for children.
☎ 26630 63633 **🕐** Open for lunch and dinner

SHOPPING

 Atrapos Worth a visit for its unusual bright orange and blue ceramic bowls and jugs, fish platters, bronze candle-holders, backgammon sets, silver jewellery and puppets which represent scenes from Greek mythology. **☎** 26630 64271

Dala's Gold Modern and traditional gold and silver jewellery. **☎** 06630 63684

Mary's Shop Good ceramics and hand-made table-cloths and embroideries at good prices. **☎** 26630 63425

Olive Wood House Souvenirs for all purses ranging from hairslides and bracelets to beautifully smooth bowls. **☎** 26630 63692

Supermarket A good selection of fresh food and local home-made wine on tap; bring your own bottle for filling – it's a bargain!

El Greco € A warm welcome awaits in this popular taverna. Friendly waiters hum along to Greek music whilst serving good value traditional food at candlelit tables. **☎** 26630 63788

Faros € New cocktail bar-cum-snack bar overlooking the beach. Internet access too. Run by a friendly family. **☎** 26630 63214

Liberty's Taverna €–€€ The owner, Angelos, serves the freshest fish, charcoal grills and delicious *paella* as well as some Corfiot specialities. Try the *tsipouro* – he calls it 'smiley water' – guaranteed by Angelos to be hangover-free! **☎** 26630 63496

Maistro €€ This large beachside restaurant manages to retain an intimate atmosphere with little oil lamps and gentle Greek music. The fresh fish is especially good. **☎** 26630 63020

The Pumphouse €–€€ You can go Greek with a delicious meatball dish like souzoukakia, take the fish route of fresh lobster and mussels, or choose a delicious selection of *mezedes*. ⓐ At the Pumphouse roundabout ☎ 26630 63271 🕐 Open for lunch and dinner

 Skondras Taverna € Lovely, friendly taverna right by the beach. Try their tasty *meze* for starters. ☎ 26630 63048

 Valentine's €€ The owner runs a restaurant in Canada in the winter, bringing his professional service and delicious dishes to Acharavi in the summer. A good place to watch the sun set over the sea. ☎ 26630 64264

NIGHTLIFE

Bellissimo Eat breakfast or have a snack, play mini-basketball, watch major sporting events on satellite TV and listen to all kinds of music from an English DJ. Don't forget to try the Bellissimo cocktail. ☎ 26630 63789

Captain Aris Bar A meeting place for everyone with a great range of drinks and snacks. This bar has a friendly, nautical atmosphere and Sky satellite TV. Captain Aris and his brother mix lethal cocktails! ⓐ Next door to Castaway Travel

Lemon Garden The large rambling lemon orchard is the exquisite setting for cocktails by candle light.

Romeo's Run by an English couple, Alan and Anita, this fun bar has a great atmosphere with quiz nights and pool competitions.

Veggera Light meals during the day, ice creams, alcoholic milkshakes, cocktails and crêpes at night. Greeks and tourists gather twice a week for the excellent Greek dancing show – a blend of old and new traditional dances. ☎ 26630 63886

Yamas The young and lively hang out here for excellent cocktails in a buzzing atmosphere.

🔺 *Kassiopi's attractive harbour was once a bustling port*

Kassiopi
lively fishing village

Kassiopi's pretty harbour was once a significant port, and the little village a much-coveted look-out post, attracting the marauding attentions of the Venetians and Turks, amongst others. Today the only invaders are the tour buses, which fill the harbour square.

THINGS TO SEE & DO
Boat trips ★★★
The Travel Corner runs a wide selection of boat tours. You can shop in style by taking an evening cruise from Kassiopi to Corfu Town or enjoy a romantic cruise along the east coast at sunset. 📞 26630 81213

Kassiopitissa Church/Byzantine Fortress ★★
Located behind the Three Brothers restaurant on the harbour, this church dates from 1590 and is said to have been built on the site of

a temple of Zeus. Walk up the path opposite the church's bell tower to the ruined Byzantine fortress. It's tangled with bracken and overgrown with wild flowers, but you'll eventually come to a gateway into the fort – follow the walls round to the left for spectacular views over Kassiopi's bay and up to Mount Pantokrator.

RESTAURANTS

 Janis €€ Large airy restaurant with an à la carte menu and several set menus including seafood and vegetarian options. There's a large open-air terrace at the back overlooking Kalamionas beach. Great for that special occasion. ⓐ On the road leading from the main square to Kalamionas beach ⓣ 26630 81082

Little Italy €€ Very popular upmarket Italian place with tasty home-made pasta and pizza. ⓐ On the road out of the town centre ⓣ 26630 81749

Porto €€ One of the oldest restaurants in Kassiopi, this bright, cool terrace with its view over the bay is the perfect spot for trying a Corfiot speciality such as *bourdetto*, chunks of fish in a tasty sauce. Specialises in excellent fish. ⓐ On the harbour near to The Travel Corner

SHOPPING

Agathi's Lace Shop A wide choice of crisp table-cloths, lace mats, crocheted waistcoats and embroidered napkins.

Aleka's Lace House Exquisite lace and embroidered table-cloths flapping in the breeze on the east of the harbour mark this traditional shop. Lace table-mats are a bargain, and you know it's the real thing as you can see the women at work.

Nikolas Bakery The queue snakes out of the door in the morning as tourists and locals flock to buy *baklava*, chocolate doughnuts and savoury ham and cheese croissants.

Kalami
secluded hide-away

A haven on the north-east coast, this horseshoe-shaped bay was once home to author Lawrence Durrell. Tourism has been handled sensitively here and Kalami retains its peaceful fishing village atmosphere.

THINGS TO SEE & DO
Walks ★★
Walk along the footpath, at the back of the White House, to **Yialiskari Bay**, a wonderful spot for swimming, or carry on to **Agni**, an unspoiled pebble bay without a hotel or apartment block in sight.

Water sports ★★
Hire a boat from **Harris Kalami Boats** or learn to water-ski with **Sakis Water Sports**. Information on both from the kiosk by the White House Taverna ① 26630 91646 ⓦ www.corfuboats.gr

RESTAURANTS & BARS

Café Kalami €€ Golden oldies with a few 1980s and 1990s hits thrown in make for a mellow evening at this attractive café bar.

Taverna Bar Kalami Beach €€ From the shade of the vine-covered terrace, enjoy delicious seafood *mezedes*, local fish or home-made bean soup. Lovely views across the little bay. ① 26630 91168

Villa Matella €€ The small stone courtyard overflows with flowers, friendliness and excellent Greek food in the evening. Fresh produce is brought down daily from the owner's garden in the mountains. ① 26630 91073

The White House Taverna €€€ Enjoy the best view of the bay from where Lawrence Durrell lived in 1935 when he wrote *Prospero's Cell*. Fresh fish is the speciality. ① 26630 91251 ⓛ Open all day

TAVERNAS IN AGNI

The tiny bay of Agni, just around the headland from Kalami, has been described as the 'gourmet heart of Greece'. Here, on the white-pebble beach, are three exceptional tavernas which are open for lunch and dinner. Free water-taxis run back and forth all evening from Kalami to Agni. It's important to book, and to take the boat marked with the taverna of your choice — otherwise you may end up in one of the others!

Taverna Agni €€–€€€ Dating back to 1851, this was built by Eleni's great grandfather. Eleni now creates culinary masterpieces: *mezedes* of succulent sweet peppers, superb courgette fritters and the plumpest of mussels, followed by wild mountain beef. ☎ 26630 91142

Taverna Nikolas €€–€€€ Genuine Corfiot village food whose flavours are rarely found outside a Greek home. *Arni lemonato* (lamb with lemons) is mouth-wateringly succulent. ☎ 26630 91243

Toula's Taverna €€–€€€ Specializes in seafood – such as grilled sea bream or lobster. The prawn pilaff is legendary, cooked to order while you sample the delicious appetisers. ☎ 26630 91350

🔻 *Kalami offers a peaceful atmosphere*

Nissaki
peaceful and relaxing

The sleepy atmosphere of this little village makes relaxation as easy as ordering your first chilled beer. No noisy discos to disturb the peace, just a sprinkling of restaurants and local shops.

BEACHES
Nissaki Bay has the smallest of the three beaches, a tiny white-pebbled cove nestling at the bottom of a steep hill. At **Kaminaki beach**, the crystal-clear water is a snorkeller's paradise. Go down the steep hill, or through the olive groves from the main road. **Krouseri** has a long pebbly beach with water sports facilities, boat trips and sunbeds.

RESTAURANTS & BARS
Anthi Taverna €€ People-watch from the vine-covered terrace, which looks out over the sparkling turquoise sea. ⓐ Nissaki Bay ⓣ 26630 91069

Dimitris €€€ With fabulous views over Kalami, this is the place for that special occasion. *Souvlaki*, lobster and oyster mushrooms are all on the menu. ⓐ Main road (Kassiopi direction) ⓣ 26630 91172 ⓛ Open 19.00–midnight

Mitsos €€ A traditional Greek family taverna with unrivalled views of the sea. ⓐ Nissaki Bay ⓣ 26630 91240 ⓛ Open all day

Nissaki Grill €€ Not the best setting, overlooking the main road, but the excellent food draws people back night after night. ⓣ 26630 91767

Panorama Bar € Simply the best view in the area from the roof. ⓐ On the main road, Krouseri

○ *Nissaki is the perfect place to relax and sunbathe*

Taverna on the Rocks €€–€€€ Watch the ever-changing shades of the sea from this lovely veranda overlooking the bay. Indulge in a seafood feast of swordfish, sole, grilled prawns and mussels or choose a tender meat dish enhanced with one of the special lemon, orange, garlic, wine or mushroom sauces. ⓐ Kaminaki ❶ 26630 91374

Vitamins Taverna €€ Friendly, family-run restaurant named after grandfather 'Vitamins'. Consistently good food served on a lovely terrace overlooking the bay. ⓐ Near to Afrodite supermarket on the main road (Corfu Town direction) ❶ 26630 91278 ● Open 10.00–midnight

SHOPPING

Supermarket Afrodite A large selection of fresh food and groceries, plus a wonderful bakery next door ⓐ On the main coastal road about 100 m (109 yd) after the church
Symposium A fabulous store of local foods and wines, and fresh rolls and croissants. ⓐ A few hundred metres south of Supermarket Afrodite ❶ 26630 91094

Barbati
olive groves and white beach

Known as the 'Riviera', this part of the north-east coast of Corfu has silvery olive groves growing to the sea, separated from it only by a wide strip of shingle, with the rocky flanks of Mount Pantokrator standing majestically as a backdrop. The beach is sheltered and offers safe bathing, making it very popular for families.

THINGS TO DO
Water sports ★★
Barbati Ski Club Parasailing, waterskiing and other activities all available on the beach. ❸ In front of Akti Barbati bar and restaurant

Boat trips with Vivi Pedalos for hire and boat trips in a caique to Agni, Aghios Stefanos, Corfu Town, Vidos, Mouse Island, etc. ❶ Call Yakkis on 6932 452739 (mobile) or drop into Taverna Glyfa to see his brother Nikolas (see opposite) ❶ Ask your rep for more details

The nearest **bakery** is just down the road at Nissaki on the main coastal road next to Supermarket Afrodite. Also, Aphrodite at the **Laundry Express Service** will wash, dry, iron and deliver your laundry for a very reasonable price. There's also a dry-cleaning service (❶ 26630 91590 ❺ Open Mon–Sat 09.00– 19.00, Sun 09.30–14.30).

RESTAURANTS & BARS
Agathi Cocktail Bar €–€€ Superb views of the sea and of Corfu Town in the distance from the terrace bar serving ice creams, cocktails and every other kind of drink. ❸ Southern side of the main street in direction of Ipsos ❶ 26630 91445

Akti Barbati Restaurant & Snack Bar €–€€ Smart lavender-blue and white is the theme on this terrace overlooking the beach, shaded by lovely old olive and oleander trees. Breakfasts, snacks, *mezedes*

and Corfiot specialities such as *pastitsada*. 🅐 On the beach opposite the Barbati Ski Club 🕿 26630 91276 🕒 Open noon–19.00

🍴 **Lord Byron Restaurant and Bar** €€ The oldest taverna in Barbati contains a treasure trove of flags from all over the world and a collection of football strips displayed behind the bar. The menu includes everything from fish fingers to lobster. This is a lively spot, especially in the evenings. 🅐 North side of the main street going towards Nissaki 🕿 26630 91577 🕒 Open all day

🍴 **Restaurant Anthi** €€ A terrace overlooks the sea at this very pleasant spot serving delicious ice creams, pizzas and fresh fish and much else besides. Unlike many restaurants, they point out on the menu which fish is frozen. 🅐 On the main street, opposite the Lord Byron 🕒 Open from 09.00 for breakfast until late

🍴 **Taverna Glyfa** €€ Two terraces overlook the sparkling sea and little coves in this romantic setting. Delicious peppered steaks, sea bass, local fresh fish and lobster in season are all on the menu. Greek dancing nights and live music every week. 🅐 Far end of main street going towards Nissaki 🕿 26630 91317 🕒 Open 09.00–late

🔻 *The sheltered beach at Barbati is ideal for families*

Ipsos
vibrant nightlife

Ipsos sits on the shore of a long shingle bay which is known as the 'Golden Mile'. During the day, the beach and water sports claim the attention of most holidaymakers. By night the resort sings out into the early hours.

THINGS TO SEE & DO
Aghios Markos ★
A left-hand fork just after Pyrgi takes you to Aghios Markos on a pretty 2-km (1½ mile) stroll into rural Corfu, along a lemon-tree-studded road, past orange orchards, wild carnations and dilapidated farm buildings. The tiny half-ruined Monastery of Christ Pantokrator sits on the hillside over the village and affords a lovely view over the countryside below. Stop for some moon juice (the potent local beer) or a simple lunch at the Panorama bar.

Boat trips ★★
Captain Homer runs two excursions by boat: one to Kassiopi, in the north, with swimming stops on the way back, the other to Benitses, Mouse Island and Vidos in the south. Both include generous amounts of barbecue food and drink. ☎ 26610 97426

Go-karting ★★
Bounce off tyre barriers and tackle hairpin bends down at the go-kart track, which is set back 50 m (54 yd) from the main coastal road, next to Bar 52 (see Nightlife on page 74).

Horse riding ★
Get off the beaten track and explore rural Corfu on horseback. Sally, the owner of the **Riders Club**, organises rides on good horses for all levels of experience from novice to old hand, so why not try something different on your holiday? ⓐ Ano Korakiana ☎ 26630 22503

Mount Pantokrator ★★★

Hire a car and drive through the olive groves to Spartilas, at the foot of Mount Pantokrator, continuing up to Strinilas, perched on the mountainside. The views are fantastic. You can visit the peak, then descend through a densely wooded valley via Eriva, Lafki and down to Acharavi. The picturesque drive through the multi-hued trees and flowers is very peaceful, with hardly a car or house in sight.

BEACHES

Ipsos beach runs parallel to the main road in a narrow strip of shingle. A few kilometres further north, **Barbati** offers an unspoiled, white-pebble beach surrounded by lush mountain scenery. If you're planning to beach-hop, the Ipsos–Kassiopi road is a beautiful drive as well as taking you past **Kaminaki**, **Kalami**, **Agni** and the picturesque harbour of **Kouloura**.

RESTAURANTS

All the following restaurants are on the main road going towards Pyrgi.

Little Italy €€ The romantic garden setting amongst pots, palm trees and hammocks is probably the prettiest dinner spot in Ipsos. Generous-sized portions of pasta and wood oven pizzas. Save room for the *tiramisu*. ☎ 26610 97720

Peking House €€–€€€ Smarter than most of the tavernas along the main drag, this is one of the better Chinese restaurants in Corfu, serving a range of delicious Cantonese and Szechuan cuisine. ☎ 26610 93646

Phoebus €€ All things to all people … Andreas cooks up authentic Greek food – you'll be hard pressed to find better *kleftiko* or *stifado* elsewhere – on one half of the terrace, whilst a chef from Yorkshire works his magic on British pub grub next door. ☎ 26610 93386 🕒 Open 18.00–midnight

Pizzeria Bonita € Attention to detail makes dining on this candlelit terrace a real pleasure. Wonderful pizzas and rich pasta dishes at low prices. ⓐ Pyrgi ☎ 26610 93293

The Viceroy €€ Spice up your holiday with a vindaloo, chicken tikka or biryani. This was the first Indian restaurant in Corfu (originally in Kontokali); the British-born owner, Bryn, brings back genuine spices from India and serves them up in several delicious combinations. ☎ 26610 90830 🕐 Open 19.00–midnight, closed Mon

SHOPPING

Moons A sort of Greek-style Habitat, with wooden hand-painted clocks, scented candles, rugs, cushions, night-lights and glassware. The ceramics are bright and attractive and there's also a trendy selection of figure-hugging lycra dresses, platform and boat shoes and stylish silver jewellery. ⓐ Main road going towards Dassia

Tina's Jewellery Another place to shop for beautiful silver bracelets and bangles, swish watches and sparkling rings. ⓐ Main road going towards Dassia

NIGHTLIFE

All the following venues are on the main road.

Bambooza Enjoy a quiet(ish) cocktail on the upstairs balcony with a view over the sea or head inside to the disco for some groovy up-to-date sounds and the latest dance music. Popular with early 20s and tour groups.

Bar 52 See and be seen in this sophisticated cocktail bar where attitude, short-as-you-dare skirts and the latest dance music are all in abundant supply.

Dinos Less rowdy than the younger bars along the front, there's still a great atmosphere here. It's a favourite with anyone whose knowledge of pop music runs out after about 1986, and with couples looking for a fun evening out which can also accommodate a toddler or two. Serves value-for-money Greek and English food. ❶ 26610 97517

Dirty Nellies One of the liveliest spots, a young 20s crowd chatters, dances and drinks with Irish hosts Ursula and Theo. Karaoke and all kinds of games, which can get very boisterous indeed. ❶ 26610 93615

Hector's Club Popular with locals and visitors alike, people of all ages party till dawn to a medley of music. Loud music, drinks and lots of dancing. ❶ 26630 93014 ❷ Opens 22.30

Lumberjacks Another very lively place that stays open till dawn with DJs and a wide range of musical styles.

The Old Tree Right by the beach, a place where you can drink, dance, or just hang out, all day and all night too.

Temple Bar In the early evening typically English food is served on a candlelit terrace overlooking the sea. From 23.30 onwards, on the other side of the road, the bar rocks, bops and boogies to the sounds of the 1970s and 1980s. One of the most popular spots in Ipsos.

● *The coastline near Ipsos is known as the 'Golden Mile'*

Dassia
water sports and entertainment

Dassia's curving bay, fringed by a long stretch of silver shingle, is home to some of the best water sports on the island. Days in Dassia are spent waterskiing, windsurfing, parascending or racing through the water. In the evening the action moves to the main road, which is lined with restaurants, bars and shops. Terraces hum with chatter and gentle music, plates smash and crash in displays of Greek dancing, cocktails are shaken, stirred and replenished. Many of the restaurants combine quality food with entertainment and the resort is lively until midnight and beyond.

THINGS TO SEE & DO
Boat trips ★★
Spend a leisurely day cruising past Nissaki, Kalami and Kouloura to Kassiopi for a spot of shopping or sightseeing, or head south to Benitses past Corfu Town. Check which boat trips are on offer at the jetties along the beach.

Cycling ★
Rent a bike from **The Corfu Mountainbike Shop**, near the Elea Beach Hotel, and explore the area. They also run several escorted tours for all levels of fitness through picturesque villages and along country lanes and donkey tracks. ☎ 26610 93344

Paintballing ★★★
Accept the combat challenge or just laze by the pool observing. Children need to be 12 years and over. ➋ Kormarie campsite ☎ 26610 97177
🕑 Open 10.00–22.00

RESTAURANTS & BARS
🍴 **Dionysos** €€–€€€ Low lighting, low music but high quality, this classy taverna offers excellent meat dishes at tables set between stone arches and pots of flowers. Leave room for the liqueur-laced desserts – they're delicious. ➌ Main road ☎ 26610 93449 🕑 Open 18.00–01.00

Etrusco €€€ Excellent international restaurant with a strong Italian flavour, perfect for a special occasion. It is well worth the effort to discover this hidden treasure. The turn-off is up the hill near to Sophia's corner, from where it is signposted. Reservations necessary.
@ Off the main road between Dassia and Ipsos **❶** 26610 93342
◷ Open 20.00–01.00

Malibu € Drink your cocktail, relax by the pool and listen to great music. **@** On the beach **◷** Open 10.00–21.00

 Shakes € Kick-start the day here with the massive Yum Yum Pigs Bum cooked breakfast (with a mini version for those who want to wear a bikini on the beach). A daytime snack menu of chip butties and omelettes gives way to more substantial family favourites – cod and chips, cottage pie and scampi – in the evening. **❶** Main road

Walnut Tree Taverna (Karydia) €€ Traditional taverna with terrace serving delicious Corfiot and Greek specialities. Very popular.
❶ On a main road **❶** 26610 93432

NIGHTLIFE

Bambola If you like a dance with your drink, head down to Bambola, which strikes a happy medium between cocktail bar and disco bar. The music is of the Madonna/Wham variety played at a level you can bop to without excluding conversation. **@** Main road

Edem Bar Very popular beach bar. Lovely natural stone and wood interior. English DJ at night. Watch the sun go down – or come up. **@** On the beach, near Elea Beach Hotel **◷** Open all day until 04.00 **❶** 26610 93013

The origins of the great Greek custom of plate-smashing range from religious and prehistoric rituals to the custom of throwing out old chipped crockery as part of a spring clean.

Summer Moments Cocktails here are served with sparklers and enough fruit to open a greengrocer's shop. ❷ At the Corfu Town end of Dassia

Viva Sophisticated but friendly, this white and pink bar attracts a young crowd for post-dinner cocktails and long drinks to great music sounds. ❶ Main road

SHOPPING

 Jewellery Shop A sparkling choice of up-market silver and gold rings, necklaces and bracelets. ❶ Opposite Dassia Chandris Hotel ❶ 26610 93291 ❷ Open 10.00–14.00 and 17.00–23.00

Just Leather Prices start low for leather belts, rising for sandals and rucksacks, higher still for smart executive briefcases. ❶ 26610 93495

Olive Wood House Backgammon boards, wind chimes, candle-holders, bowls and walking sticks – you really don't have any excuses for not taking a present home. ❶ 26610 97511

Santa Barbara Clothes Shop Fake Tommy Hilfiger and Calvin Klein T-shirts, shorts, jeans, bright casual shirts and pretty summer dresses as well as plenty of slogan T-shirts. ❶ 26610 97157

Supermarket Large store encompassing a greengrocer's, leather shop, souvenir shop, bakery, clothes and beach items. ❶ At the Ipsos end of Dassia

Supermarket As well as groceries, this sells a good selection of English books and up-to-date magazines. ❶ Under Veranda restaurant

Yannis Leather Shop A reasonably priced souvenir supermarket. Offerings include fake designer handbags, bright ceramics, leather wallets and satchels, belts, shoes and summer dresses.

Kontokali & Gouvia
typical seaside villages

The building of a new marina at Kontokali a few years ago transformed this quiet village into a busy holiday resort. It has now become a popular playground for the Greeks, as well as for British, American and German tourists, and ideally placed for trips to Corfu Town and around the north of the island.

THINGS TO SEE & DO
Ipapanti church ★
Visit the Ipapanti church in its picturesque setting at the end of a narrow causeway jutting out into Gouvia bay. Reached by the road to Kommeno, it was built under Venetian rule in 1713 by the son of a Cretan aristocrat and restored to its former glory in 1996. Look out for the two festivals celebrated at the Ipapanti church – its own feast day, on 2 February, and Aghia Marina, on 17 July.

Lagoon ★★
For a small entrance fee, a great pool and excellent facilities for children await you here. Poolside bar, crazy golf and five-a-side football too – if you have the energy. ❸ Gouvia ❶ 26610 80091 ❷ Open 10.00–18.00

BEACHES
Kontokali sits in its own little bay of fine sand and pebbles and very clean water. Cleared of weed and debris at the crack of dawn every morning, it's a Blue Flag beach with sunbeds and umbrellas for hire. The pebble beach of Gouvia lies just further north, with a view of the whitewashed church of Ipapanti opposite.

RESTAURANTS
9 Muses €€ Home-made Greek specialities and a variety of steaks with international and spicy sauces. ❸ Gouvia ❶ 26610 91924 ❷ Open 17.00–midnight

Argo €€€ Overlooking the marina in Gouvia, where snazzy yachts jostle for moorings, the Argo is modern, clean and classy with a sophisticated menu and a good – if expensive – selection of wines. ❸ Gouvia ❶ 26610 99251

Gerekos €€€ A fish feast fit for kings, or at least for the Greek prime minister, the singers and the international celebrities who frequent this quaint, intimate restaurant. It's one of the best fish tavernas on the island and well worth a splurge. ❸ Kontokali ❶ 26610 91281

Gorgona €€ Not cheap, but you're paying for the excellent fresh fish and seafood, and other imaginative dishes. ❸ Gouvia main road ❶ 26610 90261

O Makis €€ If it lives in the sea, you'll find it here – grilled, sprinkled with herbs and served with a twist of lemon. Delicious red mullet, red snapper, king prawns and grilled lobster. ❸ Kontokali ❶ 26610 91814 ❻ Open for lunch and dinner

Navigators € A favourite hangout of the British expat community, this is a 'settle in for a session' sort of place with plenty of karaoke and evening entertainment. Food is mainly English: steak pie, mixed grill, etc, with a good choice for kids. ❸ Kontokali ❶ 26610 90155

Pipilas €€ Authentic Greek and Corfiot dishes served on an attractive shaded veranda. Long established in the area, it's a pleasant spot for a romantic tête-à-tête or a laid-back, low-key dinner with friends. ❸ Kontokali ❶ 26610 91201

Roula €€–€€€ Situated on a small island overlooking Gouvia Marina, you may need to book for this superb seafood place. ❸ Gerekos island, Kontokali ❶ 26610 91382

🍴 **Zorba's Taverna** €–€€ Geraniums and a palm tree growing through the wooden veranda make this a pleasant shady spot for everything from English breakfast and hamburgers to Corfiot specialities and good grilled fish. Greek dancing weekly. ⓐ Kontokali ☏ 26610 90184

NIGHTLIFE

Archies Vibrant and loud, a live DJ winds up the volume and the atmosphere as the evening rolls on with karaoke and dancing. ⓐ Kontokali

The Beer Bucket The perfect spot for Men Behaving Badly, it's draft beer, laddishness and dancing on the bar. With live rhythm and blues bands once a week, this fun pub lets the good times roll. ⓐ Kontokali

G & M Very friendly, lively bar. Dance to the sounds of music played by Greek DJs or just sit outside and relax drinking your favourite cocktail. ⓐ Kontokali

Kingsize by Prince Greek-English DJ plays great sounds to a packed house, often until dawn. This disco is also popular with locals. ⓐ Gouvia

Whispers Wide mix of fun-lovers frequent this popular venue – mostly young and 'DDG' (drop-dead gorgeous for those in the know!). ⓐ Gouvia

🔽 *Kontokali: popular playground*

Alykes
perfect island base

Situated just north of the island's capital, the silvery-grey sandy beach at Alykes has views of mountain scenery to the north and of Corfu Town to the south. The pretty islands of Lazaretto, a former quarantine station, and Vidos, a wildlife sanctuary, adorn the bay.

The green island of **Vidos** has in the past been used as a base for Ottoman attacks in the 16th and 18th centuries. After the British left Corfu in 1864 the fortifications were destroyed and it went on to become a prison. There is said to be a tunnel, excavated by the Venetians, running from Corfu Town under the sea to Vidos as it was so strategically important for the defence of the town.

As well as several ruins on the little island, a bird sanctuary and some lovely swimming spots, there is also a Serbian mausoleum where thousands of bones belonging to the soldiers who died from disease and wounds during World War I are kept. A boat service runs from the Old Port in Corfu Town to Vidos every hour on the hour from 09.00 to midnight, returning every hour on the half-hour from 09.30 to 01.30, depending on the season.

Because of its excellent location, Alykes is a perfect base for exploring the island in a series of day trips. The popular beauty spot of **Paleokastritsa** is 23 km (14 miles) to the west, with several good restaurants and bars a few kilometres north at **Kontokali**. **Corfu Town** is just 3 km (2 miles) to the south, and the area known as the 'Disco Strip', with with bars, restaurants and discos, is just 2 km (just over a mile) away on the main road leading into the capital. The tourist office (EOT) is at
ⓐ 20 Paleokastritsa Road ⓣ 26610 37520 ⓒ Open Mon–Fri 08.00–14.00

BEACHES
You can visit the beaches and villages along the north-east coast – including Nissaki, Agni and Kassiopi – by boat. Ask your representative or any travel agent for more details.

● *Take a boat trip from Alykes to visit the beaches of the north-east coast*

RESTAURANTS

Just south of the resort on the way towards Corfu Town and the New
Port is the 'Disco Strip' on the main road (Ethnikis Antistasseos Street)
which, in addition to clubs, has some good restaurants and café bars.

Elladographia €€ Enjoy delicious mezedes and home-made
wine in a friendly atmosphere. ③ Disco Strip

Remezzo €€ Crêpes, huge mixed grills, delicious cakes and
deluxe ice creams and long, cool cocktails make this a very
popular spot. All the food is homemade, using fresh fish, vegetables
and meat bought daily from the local market. Also has a mini disco
for children and makes special birthday cakes for their parties.
③ Disco Strip ① 26610 45314 ● Open all day

Roma Pizza € Good-value Italian spaghetti and pasta bar along
the port. ③ Near to Au Bar, Disco Strip

Traverso €–€€ Restaurant bar with lovely garden offering
good Greek food and large selection of Mediterranean wines.
Try the *mezedes* with a glass of *ouzo* – or the even stronger *tsipouro*.
③ 33 Ethnikis Antistasseos Street ① 26610 43956 ● Open for dinner

NIGHTLIFE

Aperitto Good mix of modern Greek music and other European dance music in a stylish and fun atmosphere. Popular with the locals.
ⓐ Disco Strip ❶ 26610 26793

Apocalypsis One not to miss. The owners have spent a small fortune on the décor and this club rivals some in Ibiza. Music is the latest from London and the crowd loves it. ⓐ Disco Strip ❶ 26610 40345

Au Bar Has a reputation as one of the best in Greece with natural stone wall interiors. It certainly has a beautiful garden cocktail bar and great DJs and is very popular with die-hard clubbers. ⓐ 30 Ethnikis Antistasseos Street ❶ 26610 34477 🕒 Opens around midnight

Hippodrome This huge club boasts its own pool. Has everything from exotic palm trees and a chill-out zone with Greek music and food to equally exotic bar-top dancers. Entrance fee includes one drink.
ⓐ 52 Ethnikis Antistasseos Street ❶ 26610 43150 🕒 Opens around 23.00 and in the mornings for swimming, coffee, drinks and snacks

Home A trip to ultimate fun at this new-look garden. Special evenings and live music from famous DJs. ⓐ 68 Ethnikis Antistasseos Street
❶ 26610 21752

Privilege Dance to the sounds of Greek and international music till dawn. ⓐ Disco Strip ❶ 26610 34477

The Disco Strip is right on the main road out of Corfu Town and gets very busy with traffic at night. It is better to travel by bus or taxi than on foot as in some places there are no safe pavements. Also, the great Greek pastime of *kamaki* – men 'spearfishing' for foreign women – is quite prevalent here!

Achilleion Palace
imperial grace

Used as the location for the James Bond film *For Your Eyes Only*, this neo-classical palace – with its impressive gardens and lavish interior – is an interesting detour through a fragment of Corfu's history.

The elaborate villa was commissioned in 1889 by Elizabeth, Empress of Austria, who instructed two Italian architects to design a palace 'worthy of Achilles', her favourite hero from ancient Greek literature. It was completed two years later and she used it until her death in 1898 as an escape from the Hapsburg court and her domineering mother-in-law.

THINGS TO SEE

The palace ★★

Cherubs hang from every wall, Corinthian pillars spring up in the stair-
wells, gilded mirrors reflect fancy decorations. The reception hall has a
frescoed ceiling by the Italian painter, Galopi, depicting the four seasons.
There are mementoes of Kaiser Wilhelm, including the desk where he
used to plan his strategies for World War I. The Palace was used as a
hospital during World Wars I and II and the Grand Casino was housed
on the second floor until 1992. ❶ 26610 56210 ❶ Ground floor only open

From 09.00 to noon, the palace is extremely busy. If you can, get
there for when it opens at 08.00 or go in the late afternoon – the
palace stays open until 19.00 daily.

The gardens ★★★

The gardens are beautifully maintained, filled with palm trees and
wonderful flowers as well as some notable statues. You can't miss
Victorious Achilles, a huge statue weighing 4.5 tons and standing over
11 m (36 ft) tall. It was the brainchild of Kaiser Wilhelm II who wanted
to reflect his own power in Achilles' imposing stance. The Empress
Elizabeth commissioned the *Dying Achilles* from the German sculptor
Ernst Herter in 1884. It depicts Achilles attempting to pull the poisoned
arrow from his only weak spot, his right heel.

The Muses colonnade, forming the upper terrace, is decorated with
statues of the nine Muses and the three Graces. The first statue in the
far left-hand corner, next to Venus, is Apollo holding a lyre, the work of
Italian sculptor Canova. Peer through the wrought-iron door under the
colonnade to see the palace's most valuable painting, the enormous
The Triumph of Achilles by the Austrian painter, Franz Matsch.

◀ *The statue of the Dying Achilles in the gardens of Achilleion Palace*

EXCURSIONS

Albania
land of mystery

A visit to Albania used to be a popular day trip from Corfu, but then in the 1990s with fighting in the former Yugoslavia the borders came down and the trips ceased. Now, with peace in the Balkans and Albania throwing its arms open to tourists, those trips are very much on again.

Albania is only 2 km (just over a mile) away at its shortest distance from Corfu, although you will have to get up early in many parts of the island because at the moment boats only leave from Corfu Town. Most travel agents will organize a tour for you, and take care of the arrangements, like getting a visa. You don't need to worry about changing money as most Albanian places will accept euros, or the tour leader will settle the bill and you can pay them back in euros.

Some companies offer two- and three-day trips if you're really curious, but most people settle for the one-day option, which allows you plenty of time in Albania as the crossing only takes about 75 minutes. From the brand new terminal building in the port of **Sarande**, a coach will take you to enjoy a relaxing drink on the seafront promenade, about a mile away but a million miles away from most people's idea of what Albania is going to be like.

Most tours include a visit to the nearby archaeological site and national park at **Butrint**, although in some cases it is an optional extra. It is something not to be missed, however, as the 24 km (15 mile) drive there gives you a glimpse of Albania's beautiful countryside, the views across the Ionian Sea back to Corfu, and also Lake Butrint where some of the country's very tasty mussels are cultivated. Watch out at the side of the road for the old military bunkers, which the former dictator Enver Hoxha put up everywhere. Some have been amusingly decorated by Albanian artists and turned into colourful works of art.

You enter the archaeological site down an avenue which is lined with eucalyptus trees, and while the site is quite small it is very impressively situated, clustered around a hill with views over the lake. It is also rather overgrown in places, which is a refreshing change from seeing sites that are immaculately manicured. You might have to look out for snakes, though, so watch where you're walking!

Take some mosquito repellent with you, if you are visiting the archaeological site at Butrint. They're not bad enough to put you off, but they are around and can be irritating.

The remains include a theatre which could hold up to 2500 people and which is still used today for an annual summer arts festival. There are some lovely mosaics, which are often kept covered to preserve them, but your guide might be able to let you take a look. The path winds past the remains of a temple, a baptistry and other buildings, through the Lion Gate, and up to the top of the hill where you find a castle and small museum, and good views around.

From here you'll be taken somewhere for lunch, with Albanian food being an interesting mix of Greek and Turkish. With time for shopping in **Sarande**, and perhaps another drink, it's then back on board the boat for the crossing back to Corfu. Most people leave with a desire to see more of this mysterious country whose borders were closed to visitors for so long.

◗ *The archaeological site at Butrint has an impressive situation*

Parga
beautiful harbour

The attractive terracotta-roofed village of Parga huddles amongst olive groves on the Greek mainland overlooking the harbour. Pastel-coloured and white-washed houses with floral balconies line narrow alleyways, threading up into the hills behind the port. An old Venetian fort stands guard at the western end of the bay, with a tiny islet and church sitting prettily in the middle.

SHOPPING

Bakery The delicious smells escaping into the street should be more than enough to lure you in here for fresh bread, croissants, a sticky *pain au raisin*, cheese pies, cookies, cakes or sandwiches to take up to the castle for a picnic. ❸ In the street leading up to the castle, on the right after Sirenes

Distillerie Parga Family-run for over 120 years; the liqueurs are distilled to a heady 24 per cent proof. The chatty owner, Byron, will offer you free tastes of liqueurs such as banana, cherry and peppermint or a seven-year-old brandy or *ouzo*. Top buys include kumquat liqueur, which is delicious served with ice or as a topping for crêpes, or the sweet almond liqueur.

Sirenes Olive Oil Shop Pictures from the family album tracing the history of olive oil adorn the walls of this fascinating little shop. Stylish and designer-orientated, items are high quality but not cheap. Choose from ceramic olive-oil lamps, elegant conical glass jugs and beautiful dual salad dressers containing oil and balsamic vinegar. If you've overdone the tan, pick up some olive-oil soap – it's said to moisturize the skin after exposure to the sun. ❸ In the street leading up to the castle

THINGS TO SEE
Venetian Fortress ★★
Walk up to the castle for a bird's-eye view over the bay. It is crumbling and overgrown, cannon barrels lie higgledy-piggledy on the grass, butterflies dance against the blue sky and the higher levels are shaded with fir trees – ideal for a lunchtime picnic. The far side of the castle offers a wonderful panorama over the sandy Valtos beach and the craggy mountain beyond, but hold on to the children as safety barriers leave a lot to be desired. ● Open daily 09.00–21.00

BEACHES
Relax in the sun on the sand-and-shingle harbour beach of **Kryoneri** which, despite its location near the ferry boats, has clean, clear water. Enjoy the view of the islet opposite, or hire a pedalo and paddle round it.

Turn right at the jetty and follow the road round to the smaller **Golfo beach**, surrounded by rocks and *maquis* on either side.

⊘ *Parga is an attractive village on the Greek mainland*

Paxos
island hideaway

The little island of Paxos has three natural harbours. Ferries arrive at the most southerly, Gaios, the island's capital, which is protected by two little islets: the tiny Panayia, and the pine-clad islet of Aghios Nikolaos.

Aghios Nikolaos is topped by a Venetian castle dating from 1423 and an old windmill. Only 11 km (7 miles) in length, Paxos is the smallest of the main Ionian islands and the islanders are amongst the friendliest in the whole of Greece.

Paxos is a mass of silvery-green olive trees with dramatic limestone cliffs to the west. Boats from the harbour make regular trips past the tiny sister island of Antipaxos, and into the sea caves, where the sun reflecting off the pale rocks gives the water a bright, almost luminous, blue sheen.

Gaios harbour is a picturesque mish-mash of shops, tavernas and cafés where you can sit and enjoy the view. To the west is the **Governor's house**, used by the British and the Venetians. This lovely building has a faded charm and currently houses the **Gaios Folk museum** (🕐 Open 11.00–13.30 and 19.00–22.00 ❶ Admission charge).

Behind the harbour is a web of pretty streets hung with washing and flowers. Walking south (right as you face the water) along the road parallel to the harbour, you will have a pretty stroll through the olive groves. There are several little beaches along the coast with wonderfully clear water – excellent for snorkelling but look out for the sea urchins.

↘ Most excursions combine Parga and Paxos in a cruise along the eastern coast of Corfu, which is a wonderful way to see the sights of Corfu Town from the sea. Try to sit at the front of the boat – you might see dolphins playing in the water. But beware! You may just want to swim back with them to Paxos: many visitors have chosen never to leave this idyllic Greek isle.

Food & drink

Corfu's restaurants cater for an international palate, with steak, pizza and pasta featuring heavily on many menus. The larger resorts also have a fair sprinkling of English, Italian, Indian and Chinese eateries. Traditional Greek – and Corfiot – dishes are available everywhere, and the holidaymaker who steps beyond the familiar moussaka, feta cheese and taramasalata will be richly rewarded.

STARTERS

The traditional start to any Greek meal is *mezedes* – a selection of appetisers – accompanied by a glass of *ouzo*. Typical offerings will be *kalamarakia tiganita* (fried squid), *dolmadákia* (vine leaves stuffed with rice, onions and currants), *melitzanosalata* (puréed aubergines flavoured with garlic, onion, tomato and lemon juice), *taramosalata* (cod's roe dip), *skordalia* (a thick, creamy garlic dip), and *tzatziki* (a garlicky cucumber and yoghurt salad).

Hot choices are cheese *saganaki* (deep-fried chunks of regato or Kefalotiri goat's cheese), *spanakopitta* (a flaky filo pastry spinach pie), or *keftedakia* (mini meatballs). *Fasoladha* is a rich tomato, olive oil and haricot bean soup.

MAIN COURSES

Unsurprisingly, all kinds of fish are on the Corfiot menu. The menu will often just say 'fish' and the waiter will tell you which delights landed in that day's catch. *Barbouni* (red mullet), *lithrini* (sea bream) and many others are at their best simply grilled over charcoal.

Lobster is good and nowhere near as expensive as back home (it is usually priced by the kilo on menus, so check the total cost before you order). King prawns are often served as kebabs and a tasty dish for fish lovers is shrimp *saganaki* – shrimps baked in cheese and tomato sauce. *Midia yemista* (stuffed mussels baked in their shells) and *oktapodi skordato* (octopus marinated in red wine and herbs) are other delicious choices.

Meat in Corfu is tender and plentiful. There are several specialities peculiar to the island that you will find on every menu, from the simplest rural taverna to the swankiest hotel dining room. Wherever you are, be sure to try them. *Pastitsada* is traditionally cockerel meat in a tomato sauce served on a bed of spaghetti. Escalopes of veal or beef, covered in a garlic wine sauce, is the basis for *sofrito*. *Stifado* is beef stewed in a slightly spicy tomato and olive oil sauce with lots of baby onions. *Kokinisto* (chunks of beef in red wine) also makes a popular dish.

A delectable spread of typical Greek dishes

Lamb lovers will relish the spit roast, which often accompanies celebrations for saints' days, or *kleftiko* – lamb baked in a parcel of tin foil with garlic and vegetables. Simple *souvlaki* – chargrilled pork or chicken on a skewer – is a delight, usually served with rice and salad. The word *gyros* usually signifies a fast-food option of meat from a revolving spit served in pitta.

Vegetarianism is still quite a novel concept, although some of the more enlightened restaurants have a special menu. There's a reasonable amount of choice, with dishes such as *papoutsakia* – aubergines stuffed with herbs and vegetables – or *domates yemistes nistisimes* – tomatoes filled with rice, mint, onions and feta, with some places also serving meat-free *moussaka*. *Briam*, a tomato-based casserole of potatoes, courgettes, onions and green beans, and *prassopitta*, layered filo pastry filled with leeks, are tasty alternatives.

DESSERTS

Fruit is the traditional end to a Greek meal. However, for the sweet-toothed, satisfaction can be gained from the many variations of the wickedly sweet *baklava* – filo pastry stuffed with nuts and dipped in honey. Sorbets and ice creams are another popular finish to a meal, as is thick, creamy yoghurt with honey and, sometimes, nuts. Cheesecake, chocolate cake, apple pie and other standard international desserts are available in many tourist areas, albeit with a Greek twist.

DRINKS

Mezedes are traditionally accompanied by a glass of aniseed-flavoured *ouzo* which is served with chilled water. Beer drinkers will usually be offered Amstel, although the Greek lagers Mythos and Alpha are also popular. In bars geared towards the English market, beers like Newcastle Brown, Boddingtons and Caffreys are widely available.

Many restaurants serve local wine from the barrel, which is often surprisingly good. Apelia and Boutari are inexpensive, reasonable whites,

◀ *Ouzo – a traditional accompaniment to any meal*

with Tsantali turning up the quality a notch or two. Patras is a decent dry white. Good red wines are Boutari Grand Reserve, Calliga Rubis and the full-bodied Nemea.

Retsina, pine-resin-flavoured white wine, is an acquired taste. Served chilled, it's very refreshing and may well grow on you.

All the usual soft drinks – Coke, Fanta and Sprite – are sold everywhere. Ask for soda if you want sparkling mineral water. Greek coffee is served in tiny cups, complete with the grounds – so don't drain your cup. Ask for 'Nescafé' if you want something akin to coffee back home.

Expect to pay a cover charge in restaurants, which usually includes bread. Service is usually included in your bill, but it is common also to leave a tip for the waiter, or to round up the bill.

Menu decoder

Here are some of the authentic Greek dishes that you might encounter in tavernas or pastry shops.

dolmadákia Vine leaves stuffed with rice, onions and currants, dill, parsley, mint and lemon juice

domátes/piperiés yemistés Tomatoes/peppers stuffed with herb-flavoured rice (and sometimes minced lamb or beef)

fassólia saláta White beans (haricot, butter beans) dressed with olive oil, lemon juice, parsley, onions, olives and tomato

lazánia sto fourno Greek lasagne, similar to Italian lasagne, but often including additional ingredients, such as chopped boiled egg or sliced Greek-style sausages

makaronópita A pie made from macaroni blended with beaten eggs, cheese and milk, baked in puff pastry

melitzanópita A pie made from baked liquidised aubergines mixed with onions, garlic, breadcrumbs, eggs, mint and parmesan cheese

melitzano saláta Aubergine dip made from baked aubergines, liquidised with tomatoes, onions and lemon juice

mezedes A selection of appetisers, such as **tzatziki, dolmadákia** and **melitzano saláta**

moussakás Moussaka, made from fried slices of aubergines, interlayered with minced beef and béchamel sauce

pastítsio Layers of macaroni, parmesan cheese and minced meat (cooked with onions, tomatoes and basil), topped with **béchemel** sauce and baked

píta me kymá Meat pie made from minced lamb and eggs, flavoured with onions and cinnamon and baked in filo pastry

saláta horiátiki Country salad (known in England as 'Greek salad'); every restaurant has its own recipe, but the basic ingredients are tomatoes, cucumber, onions, green peppers, black olives and feta cheese, dressed with vinegar, olive oil and oregano

souvláki Kebab – usually of pork cooked over charcoal

spanakotyropitákia Cigar-shaped pies made from feta cheese, eggs, spinach, onions and nutmeg in filo pastry

taramosaláta Cod's roe dip made from puréed potatoes, smoked cod's roe, oil, lemon juice and onion

tyropitákia Small triangular cheese pies made from feta cheese and eggs in filo pastry

tzatzíki Grated cucumber and garlic in a dressing of yoghurt, olive oil and vinegar

THE KAFENEION

In Greek villages, the **kafeneion** (café) remains very much a male preserve, although visitors of both sexes will be made welcome. Customers come to read the paper, debate the issues of the day and play backgammon, as well as to consume **elinikos kafés** (Greek coffee). This is made by boiling finely ground beans in a special pot with a long handle. Sugar is added during the preparation rather than at the table, so you should order **glyko** (sweet), **metrio** (medium) or **sketo** (no sugar). In summer, try **frappé** (with ice).

Shopping

For holidaymakers used to the 'Come to my shop, just one moment, please, where are you from?' style, which accompanies many popular holiday spots, shopping Corfu style is an absolute pleasure. Most shop owners are friendly without being pushy and quite happy for you to browse in peace, but it's still worth bartering for something expensive.

CERAMICS

Ceramics are available in a wide range of shapes and finishes. Many designs are copies of museum pieces and ancient Greek pottery. Brightly coloured fruit bowls, platters and mugs are also popular.

FOOD & DRINK

Attractive herb-and-spice sets, with small bottles of olive oil or miniatures of ouzo, make good presents. Large pots of honey, with pistachios or walnuts, or the delicious pistachio cream are inexpensive alternatives. Metaxa brandy is very good, especially the five- and seven-star, and much cheaper than at home, and all supermarkets sell *ouzo*.

⊙ *The market at Benitses*

JEWELLERY

From simple beaded chokers to silver bangles and gold necklaces, there's something to suit every taste. Gold is particularly good value as the purity tends to be higher than at home – at least 14 carat, and often 18. Traditional designs include the dolphin (often seen in the waters around Corfu), and the dying Achilles statue from the Achilleion Palace.

LACE & EMBROIDERY

Embroidered cotton and lace work is of high quality in Corfu, particularly around Kassiopi where you can see old women clad in black working their threads with nimble fingers. Look out for exquisite cotton table-cloths, crocheted tops, lace table-mats and coasters at reasonable prices.

LEATHER

Fluorescent orange suede, chic leather business bags, rough-and-ready holdalls – Corfu's the place to buy a handbag for every outfit. The leather is good quality but beware – items bearing designer names are usually fake; inspect the stitching before you buy. Decent, inexpensive buys include belts, leather slippers and gloves.

OLIVE WOOD

Wonderfully smooth olive-wood souvenirs range from enormous fruit bowls and pestle-and-mortar sets to more modest hairslides and carved animals. Original designs are most likely to be found in small family-run shops with an adjacent workshop, but the labour-intensive process of smoothing by hand is reflected in high-ish prices.

OLIVES

Olive wood is so plentiful because, under Venetian rule, farmers were paid 100 pieces of silver for every 100 olive trees they planted. There are over 3 million of these silver-green trees on Corfu today.

Kids

Corfu is an ideal place for a family holiday. Children are very much part of society in Greece, and eating out is a family affair. Youngsters are well catered for in most resorts, with special children's menus – of the fish fingers and chicken nuggets variety – or small portions of mainstream Greek dishes in the more traditional tavernas. It's not unusual to see local people dining with their children well after 21.00, and no one will bat an eyelid if your toddler falls asleep in a pushchair whilst you party until midnight.

If you're sightseeing in Corfu Town and the children are flagging, revive them with a dip in the sea at **Mon Repos beach** (the far end of Garitsa Bay) or – not as clean but more central – **Alekos beach** (down a slope on the point before St Michael and St George's Palace).

WATER SPORTS

A really fun day out for all the family is a trip to **Aqualand** at Aghios Ioannis, west of Corfu Town on the Glyfada road (🕐 Open 10.00–19.00 ❶ Admission charge). The attractions include a bouncy castle, small slides and climbing frames for young children, giant twister slides, kamikaze rides – and the Black Hole for older kids and fun-seeking adults. It's wonderfully clean, with very strict safety standards and plenty of sunbeds, showers and changing rooms. The snack bars are reasonably priced too.

Smaller waterslides are available at Moraitika (although it is more cost-effective at Aqualand), Sidari and Aghios Ioannis (near Benitses).

Take to the ocean waves with one of the many boat trips. They usually include swimming stops and many visit old pirate caves. Kassiopi, Benitses and Corfu Town are popular destinations. Many water sports operators will negotiate a special price for two or more children, particularly in the low season.

It's a good idea to encourage children to have a siesta in the afternoon as dance displays and entertainment typically start around 21.30.

GO GREEK

Look out for restaurants advertising Greek dancing displays. Children are frequently invited to join in and may find themselves being balanced on the top of a table held by someone's teeth! They particularly relish plate-smashing sessions. Many hotels and bars also offer specific children's entertainment.

The **Messonghi Beach Hotel** has a team of entertainers with a whole repertoire of songs and games to keep children on their toes (ⓐ Between Moraitika and Messonghi ❶ 26610 76684). A trip to the Greek evenings at **Korakiana** and **Kynopiastes** is fun for all ages (page 107).

🔽 *Shopping with kids can be fun*

Sports & activities

After you've read a few books, supped a few beers and stopped waking up thinking you're late for work, you might fancy stretching your legs to see some of the glorious scenery Corfu has to offer. A gentle walk, a competitive game of golf or a rollercoaster bicycle ride through the hills – whatever – it's yours for the taking.

CYCLING
Cycling is an inexpensive way to explore the island. Hiring a mountain bike for the day is easy and cheap. Guided tours, which explore rural Corfu at a leisurely pace, are run by the **Corfu Mountainbike Shop** in Dassia (page 87) and **Mountain Mania** in Sidari (page 63).

GOLF
Corfu's 18-hole golf course nestles in the lush green surroundings of the Ropa Valley, 14 km (22 miles) west of Corfu Town. It's set against

● *There are many water sports on offer in Corfu*

a backdrop of thickly wooded hills with a fair sprinkling of lakes, streams and tree-lined fairways to provide challenges for experienced golfers. Beginners can take their first swings amidst the spectacular scenery – half an hour's individual tuition is reasonably priced and there are discounts for groups.

HORSE RIDING

Sit back and enjoy the countryside and let the horse take the strain. A variety of excursions on horseback for all levels of experience are available from Sidari (the **Yellow Boat Company**), Roda (**H N Travel**) and Ipsos (**The Rider's Club).**

WALKING

Even the liveliest resorts are within just a few kilometres of peaceful countryside. Olive groves, lemon orchards and paths dotted with an abundance of wild flowers await the visitor who ventures off the beaten track. Villages such as Spartilas, Strinilas, Episkepsi and Nimfes on the slopes of Mount Pantokrator offer glimpses of traditional Corfiot life, as does Ano Pavliana and the area around Aghios Mattheos.

Keen walkers should invest in a book called *The Corfu Trail* by Hilary Whitton Paipeti, which contains information about the long-distance footpath which the author created, running from the southernmost to the northernmost point of the island.

WATER SPORTS

Whichever beach you choose, you'll be inundated with opportunities to test your skill – and sometimes your nerve – in the water. Activities vary from the fairly sedate, such as canoes and pedalos, to the more dynamic waterskiing, windsurfing and parascending. You can invest in a course of ten windsurfing lessons or a ten-hour sailing course. Diving is offered in various resorts around the island. Those offering internationally recognised PADI, CMAS or BSAC qualifications are a good starting point. Please note that you should allow at least 24 hours to elapse after your dive before flying.

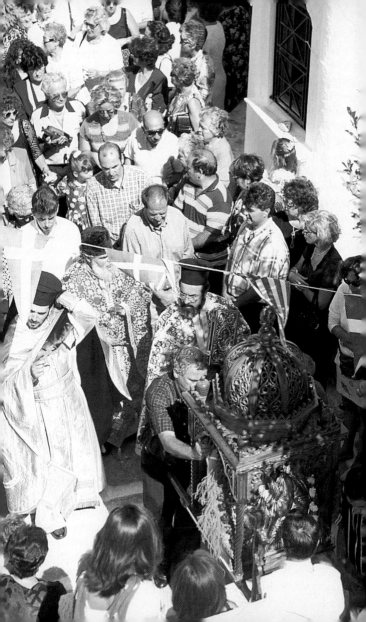

Festivals & events

GREEK NIGHTS

Dance and music are an integral part of Greek culture. Some restaurants have special Greek nights when you pay for a set menu dinner and show. Others offer dancing displays and entertainment at no extra charge.

Performed well, the various dances – *sirtaki* (better known as Zorba the Greek), *hasapiko* and *tsifteteli* (belly-dancing) – are spectacular finger-snapping, hand-clapping fun and holidaymakers will usually have a chance to learn a step or two.

Korakiana and **Kynopiastes** are the main dance venues in Corfu offering a thoroughly entertaining evening of traditional and modern Greek dance, belly-dancing, acrobatics, live singers, guitarists and *bouzouki* music (the *bouzouki* being a cross between a guitar and a banjo). The evening includes dinner and wine and can be booked from any resort on the island.

If you're in Corfu late in the year, 28 October is Ochi Day – an unashamedly patriotic national holiday with processions and dancing to commemorate the Greek Prime Minister's reply to Mussolini's call for Greek surrender in 1940 – No! (Ochi!)

ORTHODOX EASTER

Easter is the most important date in the Greek Orthodox calendar and can fall up to three weeks either side of the British Easter. Corfu Town is the place to be on Easter Saturday morning when you can see people throwing pots and crockery from their balconies (symbolizing a fresh start to the year).

In the evening, after mass, there is a spectacular firework display before everyone goes home to eat a special lamb and vegetable soup called *mayeritsa*.

◀ *Festival of the Assumption*

SAINTS' DAYS

Everyone in the Greek Orthodox church is named after a saint, and they celebrate their saint's feast day rather than their birthday. Throughout the year every village celebrates its church's name day. Many of these fall in the summer, so look out for the festivals, dancing and drinking which accompany them, but remember that much of the partying takes place on the evening before the actual day.

Some common saints' days to watch out for are 23 April, St George's Day, 29 June, St Peter and St Paul's day and 17 July, St Marina's day, which is widely celebrated in rural villages as she is the protector of crops. The Assumption of the Virgin Mary, on 15 August, is the most important day after Easter – it is a national holiday, when all the shops are closed.

The pretty Barcarola festival takes place in Garitsa Bay on 10 August. The street lamps are switched off, and floats decorated with fairy lights and candles illuminate the sea. Greek musicians and local dance schools performing in the streets add to the carnival atmosphere.

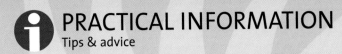

PRACTICAL INFORMATION
Tips & advice

Preparing to go

GETTING THERE

The cheapest way to get to Corfu is to book a package holiday with one of the leading tour operators specializing in Greek island holidays. You should also check the Travel supplements of the weekend newspapers, such as the *Sunday Telegraph* and *The Sunday Times*. They often carry adverts for inexpensive flights, as well as classified adverts for privately owned villas and apartments to rent in most popular holiday destinations.

If your travelling times are flexible, and if you can avoid the school holidays, you can also find some very cheap last-minute deals using the websites for the leading holiday companies. Further information about Corfu can be obtained from the Greek Tourism Organisation.

ⓐ 4 Conduit Street, London W1S 2DJ ❶ 0207 495 9300
ⓕ 0207 287 1369 Ⓦ www.gnto.co.uk

BY AIR

There are numerous charter companies offering flights to Corfu during the summer months, though if you travel out of season, you may have to use a scheduled international flight to Athens and then take an internal flight on Olympic Airways, the Greek national airline (Olympic's UK office is at ⓐ 11 Conduit Street, London W1S 2LP ❶ 0870 606 0460 ⓕ 020 7493 0563 Ⓦ www.olympicairways.co.uk). If you can be flexible about when you visit, you can pick up relatively inexpensive special deals. As a rule, the further in advance you buy your ticket, the cheaper it usually is – but you can also get good last-minute deals from on-line travel agents via the internet.

BEFORE YOU LEAVE

Holidays should be about fun and relaxation, so avoid last minute panics and stress by making your preparations well in advance.

It is not necessary to have inoculations to travel in Europe, but you should make sure you and your family are up to date with the basics, such as tetanus. It is a good idea to pack a small first-aid kit to carry with you containing plasters, antiseptic cream, travel sickness pills, insect repellent and/or bite relief cream, antihistamine tablets, upset stomach remedies and painkillers.

Sun lotion can be more expensive in Corfu than in the UK so it is worth taking a good selection especially of the higher factor lotions if you have children with you, and don't forget after-sun cream as well.

If you are taking prescription medicines, ensure that you take enough for the duration of your visit – you may find it impossible to obtain the same medicines in Corfu. It is also worth having a dental check-up before you go.

DOCUMENTS

The most important documents you will need are your tickets and your passport. Check well in advance that your passport is up to date and has at least three months left to run (six months is even better). All children, including newborn babies, need their own passport now, unless they are already included on the passport of the person they are travelling with. It generally takes at least three weeks to process a passport renewal. This can be longer in the run-up to the summer months. For the latest information on how to renew your passport and the processing times call the Passport Agency on 0870 521 0410, or access their website ⓦ www.ukpa.gov.uk

You should check the details of your travel tickets well before your departure, ensuring that the timings and dates are correct.

If you are thinking of hiring a car while you are away, you will need to have your UK driving licence with you. If you want more than one driver for the car, the other drivers must have their licence too.

MONEY

You will need some currency before you go, especially if your flight gets you to your destination at the weekend or late in the day after the banks have closed. Traveller's cheques are the safest way to carry money because the money will be refunded if the cheques are lost or stolen. To buy traveller's cheques or exchange money at a bank you may need to give up to a week's notice, depending on the quantity of foreign currency you require. You can exchange money at the airport before you depart. You should also make sure that your credit, charge and debit cards are up to date – you do not want them to expire mid holiday – and that your credit limit is sufficient to allow you to make those holiday purchases. Don't forget, too, to check your PIN numbers in case you haven't used them for a while – you may want to draw money from cash dispensers while you are away. Ring your bank or card company for help.

INSURANCE

Have you got sufficient cover for your holiday? Check that your policy covers you adequately for loss of possessions and valuables, for activities you might want to try – such as scuba-diving, horse-riding, or water sports – and for emergency medical and dental treatment, including flights home if required.

After January 2006, a new EHIC card replaces the E111 form to allow UK visitors access to reduced-cost, and sometimes free state-provided medical treatment in the EEA. For further information, ring EHIC enquiries line (☎ 0845 605 0707), or visit the Department of Health website (Ⓦ www.dh.gov.uk).

CLIMATE

The weather on Corfu is generally good. There is always the possibility of a windy spell or a short burst of rain, but this won't last more than a day or two. July and August are the hottest months and the temperature can occasionally reach 40°C (104°F). The climate table below will give you more information on the weather.

May	Day 20–26°C (68–79°F)	Night 15–22°C (59–72°F)
June	Day 25–30°C (77–86°F)	Night 19–26°C (66–79°F)
July	Day 31–38°C (88–100°F)	Night 23–30°C (74–86°F)
Aug	Day 30–36°C (86–97°F)	Night 22–29°C (72–85°F)
Sept	Day 27–32°C (81–90°F)	Night 20–27°C (68–81°F)
Oct	Day 21–28°C (70–83°F)	Night 17–23°C (63–74°F)

During the day in May and October you can wear skirts and shorts and short sleeves but in the evening you will need a cardigan or jacket because the temperature drops. In June, July, August and September you can wear shorts, skirts and strappy or sleeveless tops. At night it might get a bit chilly so you may need a light cardigan.

SECURITY

Take sensible precautions to prevent your house being burgled while you are away:

- Cancel milk, newspapers and other regular deliveries so that post and milk does not pile up on the doorstep, indicating that you are away.
- Let the postman know where to leave parcels and bulky mail that will not go through your letterbox – ideally with a next-door neighbour.
- If possible, arrange for a friend or neighbour to visit regularly, closing and opening curtains in the evening and morning, and switching lights on and off to give the impression that the house is occupied.
- Consider buying electrical timing devices that will switch lights and radios on and off, again to give the impression that there is someone in the house.
- Let Neighbourhood Watch representatives know that you will be away so that they can keep an eye on your home.
- If you have a burglar alarm, make sure that it is serviced and working properly and is switched on when you leave (you may find that your insurance policy requires this). Ensure that a neighbour is able to gain access to the alarm to turn it off if it is set off accidentally.
- If you are leaving cars unattended, put them in a garage, if possible, and leave a key with a neighbour in case the alarm goes off.

TELEPHONING CORFU

To call Corfu from the UK, dial 00 30 followed by the nine-digit number.

AIRPORT PARKING AND ACCOMMODATION

If you intend to leave your car in an airport car park while you are away, or stay the night at an airport hotel before or after your flight, you should book well ahead. Airport accommodation gets booked up several weeks in advance, especially during the height of the holiday season. Check whether the hotel offers free parking for the duration of the holiday – often the savings made on parking costs can significantly reduce the accommodation price.

PACKING TIPS

Baggage allowances vary according to the airline, destination and the class of travel, but 20kg (44lb) per person is the norm for luggage that is carried in the hold (it usually tells you what the weight limit is on your ticket). You are also allowed one item of cabin baggage weighing no more than 5kg (11lb), and measuring 46 by 30 by 23cm (18 by 12 by 9 inches). In addition, you can usually carry your duty-free purchases, umbrella, handbag, coat, camera, etc, as hand baggage. Large items – surfboards, golf-clubs, collapsible wheelchairs and pushchairs – are usually charged as extras and it is a good idea to let the airline know in advance that you want to bring these.

CHECK-IN, PASSPORT CONTROL AND CUSTOMS

First-time travellers can often find airport security intimidating, but it is all very easy really.

- Check-in desks usually open two or three hours before the flight is due to depart. Arrive early for the best choice of seats.
- Look for your flight number on the TV monitors in the check-in area, and find the relevant check-in desk. Your tickets will be checked and your luggage taken. Take your boarding card and go to the departure gate. Here your hand luggage will be X-rayed and your passport checked.
- In the departure area, you can shop and relax, but watch the monitors that tell you when to board – usually at least 30 minutes before take-off. Go to the departure gate shown on the monitor and follow the instructions given to you by the airline staff.

During your stay

AIRPORTS

Your holiday rep will give you necessary details, but here are the basics. Check-in desks usually open two to three hours before the flight. If you are flying on a Monday or Friday (which are the busiest days) you will have to prepare yourself to cope with queueing for a substantial amount of time before you finally reach the check-in desk. After your tickets have been checked and your luggage taken, you can relax, have a snack or drink at the restaurant or do any last minute shopping.

Watch the monitors that tell you when to board – usually about 30 minutes before take-off – and listen to the announcements that will inform you of any delays or other changes and remind you of the departure time and gate.

BEACHES

In summer, many beaches have life guards and a flag safety system. Make sure you understand the local signalling code (your rep or someone at your hotel will help you). Other beaches may be safe for swimming but there are unlikely to be lifeguards or life-saving amenities available. Bear in mind that the strong winds that develop in the hotter months can quickly change a safe beach into a not-so-safe one, and some can have strong currents the further out that you go. If in doubt, ask your local representative or at your hotel. Remember that you should never swim after eating a heavy meal or after drinking alcohol.

BEACH SAFETY
Most beaches where the public bathe in numbers operate a flag system to indicate the sea conditions.
- Red (or black): dangerous – no swimming
- Yellow: good swimmers only – apply caution
- Green (or white): safe bathing conditions for all

CHILDREN'S ACTIVITIES

There is plenty for children to do in Corfu. They will certainly enjoy a visit to the two big waterparks, Aqualand or Hydropolis. If your children feel brave enough, they can even try snorkelling or windsurfing. Go-karting and horse-riding are available and if they are over 12 they will love playing the ultimate combat game, paint-ball. Many hotels offer entertainment for children and organize events and games for them.

CONSULATE

The British Consulate is situated at 1 Menekratous Street in Corfu Town and the consul will be happy to help you with anything you may need.
❶ 26610 30055 ● Open Mon–Fri 09.00–13.00

CURRENCY

When Greece adopted the euro in 2002 prices were rounded up, but things like cigarettes, food, refreshments, etc., are still less expensive than in the UK. Euro (€) note denominations are 5, 10, 20, 50, 100, 200, 500 euro. Coins are 1 and 2 euro and 1, 2, 5, 10, 20 and 50 cents. However, it is inadvisable to carry 100, 200 and 500 euro notes. No one will accept a 200 euro note to pay for a phonecard.

Exchange Most of the banks are in Corfu Town, with an increasing number in the resorts around the island. Changing money is not a problem. ● Banks are open Monday to Friday 08.30–13.30. There are also 24-hour ATMs in large resorts.

Credit cards Most restaurants and large shops accept credit cards. Cafés and bars are cash only.

CUSTOMS

Numerous processions with singers and sometimes a philharmonic band take place during the summer in every village on the day of its patron saint. The processions are followed by a *panegyri* (local feast) where traditional spit-roasted lamb is eaten and you can try local dancing. If you visit Corfu early in the season, you might be there during Easter. The

Corfiot Easter is spectacular and attracts crowds from all over Greece. Visit the monasteries in Kanoni or Platytera and listen to byzantine hymns or stay in Corfu Town on Good Friday and follow the processions that leave from each church.

ELECTRICITY

The voltage in Greece is 220V. You will need a European two-pin adaptor in order to use any appliances you bring with you from the UK. Adaptors are readily available from electrical shops or at the airport.

FACILITIES FOR THE DISABLED

In the past, facilities for the disabled were almost non-existent in Corfu, although things are getting better. People have begun to realize the importance of caring for the disabled. Most hotels now have disabled facilities and they are being installed in public places.

GETTING AROUND

Car hire and driving If you want to explore the island by yourself, the best way is to hire a car, which is very affordable in Corfu. To hire a car you must hold a full driving licence and be over 21. You will be asked to leave a credit card swipe to cover any additional charges that might occur. Read the terms on the contract thoroughly and make sure you have a breakdown number in case anything untoward happens. Refuelling, damaged tyres, broken lights, etc., will be charged extra. Give yourself plenty of time to get used to driving on the right. The roads are generally good but watch out for hairpin bends and ditches at the side of the road (usually uncovered). Minor roads in the mountains and by the more isolated beaches tend to be unpaved boneshakers, so bear in mind that car insurance in Corfu doesn't include the tyres. Signs everywhere are in Greek and English. Speed limits are 50 km/h (32 mph) in built-up areas, 80 km/h (50 mph) elsewhere. Every year there are fatalities involving tourists who have hired mopeds. If you must rent a moped, make sure you wear a helmet.

Public transport Public transport in Corfu is quite good and there is a frequent bus service to all major resorts and villages.The bus service is good and cheap (pay on the bus), although it's often standing room only in high season. Blue buses serve the local area around Corfu Town – Kontokali, Perama, Kanoni, etc. – and arrive/depart from San Rocco Square. Green buses (☎ 26610 39862) serve resorts further afield – Sidari, Liapades, Ipsos, Acharavi – arriving and departing from Avramiou Street (one street down from the New Fortress). Although the bus system is very Corfu Town-focused, some of the larger resorts such as Sidari and Kassiopi are connected by a more infrequent service. Services on a Sunday are generally very limited or non-existent.

Taxis These are metered but get one from a taxi rank rather than phoning for one – the meter starts ticking as soon as the driver receives your phone call (☎ 26610 33811). Taxi drivers are usually honest, but it's worth checking roughly how much the journey will cost before you get in. Short journeys are relatively inexpensive, longer trips can be pretty hefty.

HEALTH MATTERS

In addition to the E111 form or equivalent you can purchase holiday insurance which will cover everything from the loss of your passport and to repatriation expenses. Check that any policy you take out covers you for activities such as scuba-diving, horse-riding and water sports, if you intend to try these. If the worst happens and you get a toothache or food poisoning, the General State Hospital is in Corfu Town (☎ 26610 45811) and there are a number of private clinics and a full range of specialised doctors who speak good English in the principal tourist areas.

Health hazards Too much sun can result in dehydration, so avoid sunbathing during the hottest time of the day, drink plenty of water and never go out without wearing a high-factor cream. At the first sign of sunburn, stop immediately, take a cool shower and apply after sun cream. Always wear a hat when you are walking to protect yourself. Sunstroke is one of the commonest ailments to affect holidaymakers on Corfu. Don't underestimate the strength of the sun, even on windy days, and take advantage of the umbrellas available for rent on the beaches.

Water Tap water is safe to drink but water is readily available from supermarkets, bars, restaurants or kiosks everywhere on the island.

Pests Watch out for sea urchins on rocky beaches – if you're unlucky enough to tread on one, a sterilised needle is the answer. Mosquitoes on Corfu are hungry for pale-skinned tourists during the summer months. Keep them on a diet by applying plenty of repellent and investing in a plug-in machine that releases mozzie-zapping vapours during the night.

Doctors The large resorts have 24-hour surgeries with at least one English-speaking doctor.

Pharmacies Can help with minor ailments, with antibiotics dished out more freely (i.e. without prescription) than back home. (Closed for lunch and on Sundays).

THE LANGUAGE

A difficult language, the beauty of Greek is that it is phonetic. Greeks love to hear visitors attempt to speak it. However, most signs are in Greek and English, and English is so widely – and well – spoken that you can happily trundle through a fortnight without needing a word of Greek.

THE GREEK ALPHABET

Greek	Name	Pronounced
Α α	alpha	a
Β β	beta	b
Γ γ	gamma	g, but becomes y in front of e and i
Δ δ	delta	d
Ε ε	epsilon	e as in extra
Ζ ζ	zeta	z
Η η	eta	e as in eat
Θ θ	theta	th
Ι ι	iota	i
Κ κ	kappa	k
Λ λ	lamda	l
Μ μ	mi	m

Greek	Name	Pronounced
Ν ν	ni	n
Ξ ξ	xi	x
Ο ο	omicron	short o
Π π	pi	p
Ρ ρ	rho	r
Σ σ	sigma	s
Τ τ	taf	t
Υ υ	ypsilon	u
Φ φ	phi	ph
Χ χ	chi	ch as in loch
Ψ ψ	psi	ps
Ω ω	omega	long o

 PRACTICAL INFORMATION

ENGLISH	GREEK (pronunciation)
General vocabulary	
yes/no	*neh/Okhee*
please/thank you	*parakahLO/efkhareesTO*
hello/goodbye	*YAsoo/andEEo*
good morning	*kahleeMEHRa*
good afternoon/evening	*kahleeSPEHRa*
good night	*kahleeNEEKHtah*
OK	*enDACKsee*
excuse me/sorry	*signomEE*
Help!	*Voylthia!*
today/tomorrow	*siMEHRa/AHvrio*
yesterday	*ekTES*

Useful words and phrases	
open/closed	*anikTON/klisTON*
right/left	*thexiA/aristerA*
How much is it?	*POso kAni?*
Where is a bank/post office?	*Poo Ine i TRApeza?/to tahithromEEo?*
Where is the bus station?	*Poo Ine o stathMOS ton iperastiKON leoforEEon?*
stamp	*grammatOseemo*
doctor/hospital	*YAHtros/nosokoMEEo*
police	*assteenoMEEa*
I would like...	*Tha Ithela...*
menu	*menOO*
toilets	*tooahLEHtess*
mineral water	*emfialoMENo nerO*
bread	*psomEE*
salt/pepper	*alAHti/pipEri*
fish/meat	*psarEE/krEas*
beer/wine	*bEEra/krasEE*
Cheers!	*Steen eeyEEa soo!/YAHmas!*

ENGLISH	**GREEK** (pronunciation)

Useful words and phrases (continued)

coffee with milk	*kafEs (me gAla)*
Can we have the bill, please?	*Mas fErnete ton logariasmO, parakalO?*
I don't understand/	*then katalaVENo/*
Do you speak English?	*MilAteAnglikA?*

MEDIA

The Corfiot is an English-language newspaper issued in Corfu, where you can read local news and learn about events taking place during the month. You should be able to find it in any newsagent or big supermarket around Corfu. If you carry a radio with you, you can listen to the latest international music hits on Star (88.8FM), Life (102.9FM) or Heart Radio (94.8FM). The two local television channels are Corfu Channel and Telekerkyra, however neither of them covers the whole island. There are of course the national channels, which broadcast all over Greece and include foreign-language news. If you are worried you will miss your favourite shows during your holiday, you can rest assured. Most of the hotels and bars now offer cable television where you can watch all the latest movies too.

🔻 *The Canal D'Amour, Sidari*

OPENING HOURS

Banks Banks are open Monday to Thursday, 08.00–14.00 (13.30 on Fridays) and are closed during the weekend and bank holidays.

Restaurants Many stay open all day, from early morning till late at night.

Shops Most shops open 08.00–14.00, close for lunch and then open again 17.00–22.00, but in tourist centres, most of the shops – especially tourist shops – stay open all day. In Corfu Town shops close at 14.00 on Mondays, Wednesdays and Saturdays, reopening at 17.30 on Tuesdays, Thursdays and Fridays, although many jewellers' and tourist shops are open all day. Ordinary shops are closed on Sundays.

Museums Usually open Tuesday to Sunday 08.30–15.00.

PERSONAL COMFORT AND SECURITY

In Corfu, you must never throw toilet paper in the toilet bowl. The sewage system in Greece cannot cope with paper. Do as the Greeks do and dispose of it in the bins provided. Public toilets are few (most of them in Corfu Town), but you can always go to a restaurant or bar and use the facilities there. Most resorts offer laundry and dry-cleaning services that are generally good and quite cheap.

Personal safety in Corfu is rarely an issue. Even a woman on her own is unlikely to be hassled but take the same precautions you'd take back home. Don't walk around unlit streets late at night; don't carry large amounts of money; don't leave valuables in your car or unattended on the beach. Although petty crime isn't a big problem, it's a good idea to rent a safety-deposit box at your apartment or hotel. If you are unlucky, report your loss to the police and obtain a report to support your insurance claim.

If you come across a sign with a crossed-out camera, be extra careful as this indicates 'sensitive' areas such as airports, military bases, etc. where you are not allowed to take any pictures.

EMERGENCY NUMBERS

Ambulance 166   **Police** 100   **Fire** 199

POST OFFICES

Post The main post office is in Corfu Town (ⓐ Corner of Alexandras Street and Zafiropoulou ⓣ 26610 39604 ⓒ Open Monday to Friday 07.30–20.00). However, you will find that anywhere that sells postcards often sells postage stamps. Post boxes are yellow (ordinary post) or red (express mail).

RELIGION

The majority of the Corfiots are Christian Orthodox, but there is also a large Catholic community because of the many years Corfu was under Venetian rule. Corfu Town and the countryside are full of churches devoted to different saints. The most important one is the Saint Spiridon church in Corfu Town where the body of Saint Spiridon, the patron saint of Corfu, is placed in a silver-plated reliquary. His body – which has remained intact – was brought to Corfu from Constantinople in 1453. There is a local belief that every night Saint Spiridon leaves the church and walks through the narrow streets of town.

TELEPHONES

You can make calls from most newspaper kiosks – the call is metered and you pay when you have finished. Blue public call boxes are cheaper for overseas calls; to use one you'll need an OTE telephone card (*tilekarta*), which costs €3.00 and can be bought at most newspaper kiosks and newsagents.

For international telephone information, phone 162; and for local telephone information, phone 131.

TELEPHONING ABROAD

To call an overseas number, dial 00 (the international access code), then the country code (UK=44), then the area code minus the initial zero, followed by the number. Don't forget that Greece is two hours ahead of the UK.

TIME DIFFERENCES

Don't forget that Greece is two hours ahead of the UK. So, before you go ahead and call all your friends and family back home to tell them what a wonderful time you are having and make them jealous, remember to check your watch first.

TIPPING

Tipping is usual in Greece. You will be expected to leave something around 10 per cent for good service. If the amounts are small, a little more will be most welcome.

WEIGHTS AND MEASURES

Imperial to metric

1 inch = 2.54 centimetres
1 foot = 30 centimetres
1 mile = 1.6 kilometres
1 ounce = 28 grams
1 pound = 454 grams
1 pint = 0.6 litres
1 gallon = 4.6 litres

Metric to imperial

1 centimetre = 0.4 inches
1 metre = 3 feet, 3 inches
1 kilometre = 0.6 miles
1 gram = 0.04 ounces
1 kilogram = 2.2 pounds
1 litre = 1.8 pints

 INDEX

ACKNOWLEDGEMENTS

We would like to thank all the photographers, picture libraries and
organisations for the loan of the photographs reproduced in this book,
to whom copyright in the photograph belongs:
B and E Anderson (pages 5, 26, 42, 86);
Donna Dailey (page 85);
Jupiter Images Corporation (pages 40, 108, 125);
Pictures Colour Library (pages 11, 60, 67, 95, 96, 103, 106, 121);
Michel Setboun/Corbis (page 89);
Spectrum Colour Library (pages 35, 38, 49, 54, 69, 71, 81);
Thomas Cook Tour Operations Ltd (pages 1, 9, 16, 28, 64, 75, 83, 91, 93, 100, 104).

We would also like to thank the following for their contribution to this series:
John Woodcock (map and symbols artwork);
Becky Alexander, Patricia Baker, Sophie Bevan, Judith Chamberlain-Webber,
Nicky Gyopari, Stephanie Horner, Krystyna Mayer, Robin Pridy (editorial support);
Christine Engert, Suzie Johanson, Richard Lloyd, Richard Peters, Alistair Plumb,
Jane Prior, Barbara Theisen, Ginny Zeal, Barbara Zuñiga (design support).

Send your thoughts to
books@thomascook.com

- Found a beach bar, peaceful stretch of sand or must-see sight that we don't feature?
- Like to tip us off about any information that needs a little updating?
- Want to tell us what you love about this handy, little guidebook and more importantly how we can make it even handier?

Then here's your chance to tell all! Send us ideas, discoveries and recommendations today and then look out for your valuable input in the next edition of this title. And, as an extra 'thank you' from Thomas Cook Publishing, you'll be automatically entered into our exciting monthly prize draw.

Send an email to the above address or write to:
HotSpots Project Editor, Thomas Cook Publishing, PO Box 227,
Unit 15/16, Coningsby Road, Peterborough PE3 8SB, UK.